ZONE-TRADER PHILOSOPHY

Matthew Dwyer Reynolds

Table of Contents

BIO

Matthew Dwyer Reynolds was born on November 30, 1975 at St. Joseph's Hospital in Elmira, New York. I attended Booth Elementary School, Ernie Davis Junior High School, and Elmira Free Academy High School graduating in 1994. I then attended Corning Community College in 1994 – 1996 and participated on the Baseball team in 1995. Then I moved to Cincinnati, and attended Cincinnati State College for one quarter, then I transferred to the University of Cincinnati in January of 1997, and walked onto the Baseball team red-shirted in the spring of 1997 and then played the following year in 1998. After finishing my undergraduate in Business I transferred to Northern Kentucky University and finished up my Bachelor Degree in Finance. After finishing up my degree I then moved to Los Angeles, CA after obtaining my Series 3 license in Reno, NV, and worked for Excel Futures, Global Futures, and CybertaCTA as commodities broker prior to moving into the trading side of the business and developing my own proprietary trading methodology, after leaving CybertaCTA the third and final Introducing Broker that I worked for. I then started my own corporation called Derivative Concepts Inc. in Nevada, and continued to develop my proprietary trading methodology called Zone-Trader Philosophy, and went back to school in 2006 -2007 at the University of Phoenix, Pasadena, CA campus and received my MBA. I have written 3 articles for Futures Magazine the last called Pinpointing Entries Across Multiple Time Frames in 2008. I have run 2 live trading rooms the first called D.C. Zone-trading on Hotcomm, and the second called Futurestalk which used Hotcomm then Omnovia. I also wrote a newsletter called Cosmic Speculator as well which posted and audited live account record of over 495% return over an 18 month period.

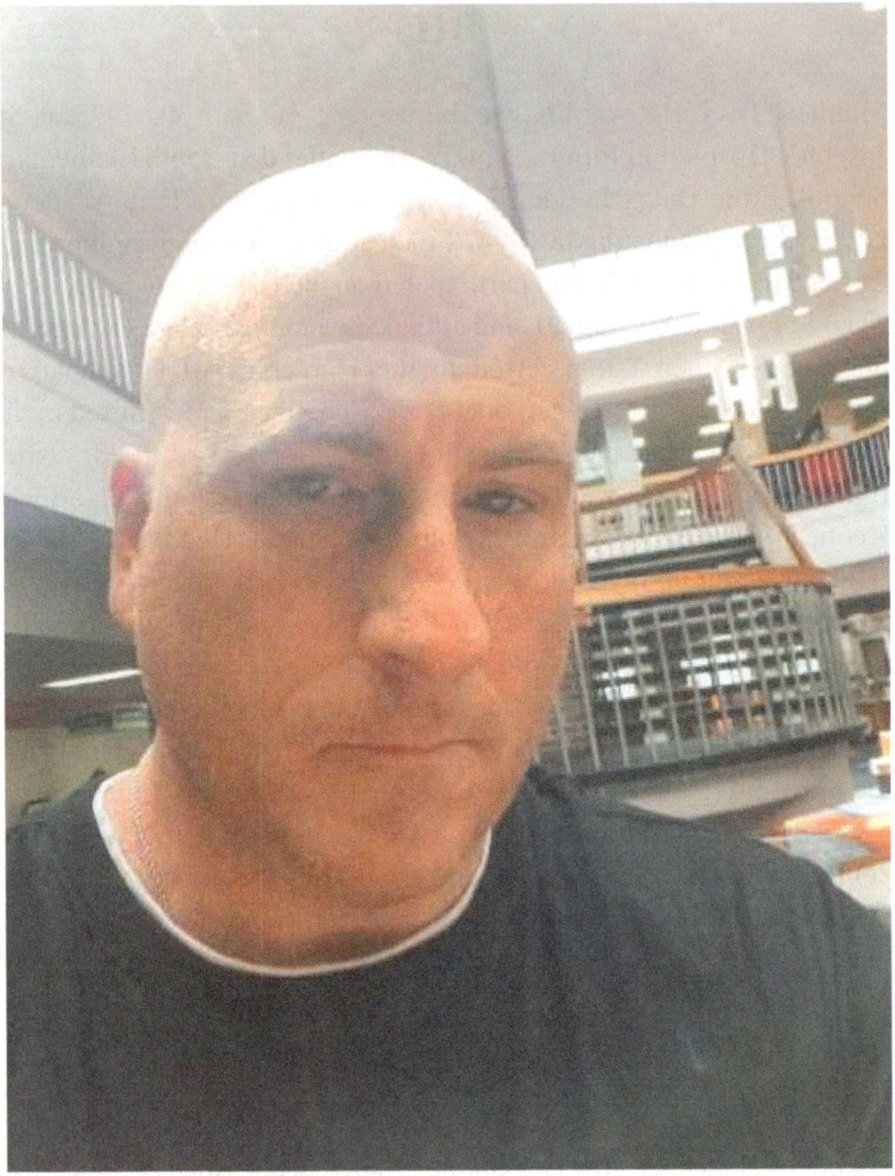

ZONE-TRADER PHILOSOPHY

Fibonacci ratios are .382, .618, .786, 1.272, 1.414, 1.618, 2.618 and are multiplied times the difference of 2 highs and 2 lows. Fibonacci (Leonardo Pisano) ratios and number sets appear in many things. He studied nature and reproduction to create his number sequence. He began with 1, 1 and added to get 2 then the last two numbers are added together to get the next so 3, 5, 8, 13, 21, 34, 55, 89, 144, 233… and so on and so forth. In Pythagoras's possessions when he died there was a triangle of course, but written inside it were Fibonacci ratios with the words "The Secret to the Universe". Fibonacci numbers in nature occur over and over again and it is not a coincidence in my belief. There are 3 primary colors. A music octave is 8. There are 8 white keys on the piano, 5 black and added together equal 13. There are 5 major senses in humans. The business cycle is 55 years. The normal sunflower has 89 curves, 55 in one direction and 34 in the opposite. The great pyramid has 5 sides and 8 borders added together to create 13. The Pyramids total height is 5,813 inches and the Egyptian standard unit of measurement is the inch, and the ratio of the base to the peak is (.618). If you divide the total amount of female bees by the total amount of male bees within a hive, the summation will arrive at or near 1.618, which is known as the golden ratio.

"Some traders believe that the Fibonacci numbers and ratios created by the sequence play an important role in finance that traders can apply using technical analysis. The golden ratio of 1.618, important to mathematicians, scientists, and naturalists for centuries is derived from the Fibonacci sequence. The quotient between each successive pair of Fibonacci numbers in the sequence approximates 1.618, or its inverse 0.618" (Investopedia.com).

The Fibonacci sequence can have an effect human behavior, in regard to trading financial instruments. The Fibonacci sequence has been utilized for years to help identify patterns in the application of technical analysis through the use of charts. Zone-trader Philosophy created by me Matthew Dwyer Reynolds born November 30, 1975 at

St. Joseph's Hospital in Elmira, NY is the first completely dynamic 100% Fibonacci based trading methodology. The main ratios that I focus on are the golden mean and its inverses, which are .618, 1.618, and 2.618, these are what I have found to be the most important ratios to focus on. The ratios are utilized to create any and all of the support and resistance levels within my 3 distributions which reside within each of my 5 profiles.

Support and Resistance is a leading indicator when utilized for application of technical analysis, if and only if the trader can determine if the support or resistance is going to hold. By combining support and resistance with candlestick patterns I was able to highly increase the ability to determine whether or not the support or resistance was going to hold and or whether the market was doing to change directions on 5 time frames, which are the Yearly which uses weekly candles, the Quarterly which uses daily candles, the monthly which uses a 377 minute candle which is also a Fibonacci ratio, the weekly profile which uses an 89 minute candle and a daily profile which uses an 8 or 13 minute candle.

IF the trader prefers to use tick charts or volume based charts then I suggest figuring out a Fibonacci sequence number that when divided into the total daily, weekly, or monthly volume it will mimic the price movement and amount of waves being created within the time charts. Keep in mind that one full wave requires price movement in either the bullish or bearish direction and then for a retracement in opposition of that original price movement that does not exceed 100% and then for the market to again resume the direction of the original movement and make either new highs or new lows.

The ability to create and or utilize a dynamic trading methodology is or can be the most important factor for creating the ability to becoming a successful trader and posting a higher than the norm winning percentage, which is what all traders know leads to consistently higher profits annually. Dynamic trading means that the methodology or the strategy has the capability to adapt to any and all current and any or all changes in the underlying condition of the market. In other words the ability to adapt to the condition of the market means that the methodology or strategy listens to and hears what the market is telling traders is going on.

Now let's take a step back and think about this more on another level, if Fibonacci mathematics is the base of my trading methodology and Leonardo Pisano's mathematics are found throughout space and nature and are considered to be the rhythm of the Universe, then that would mean that the philosophy derived from my trading methodology that explains any and all market movement being derived from the underlying condition of the market and any changes within can be considered to be the rhythm of the market.

This is the secret to the trading universe and is the reason why my trading methodology Zone-trader Philosophy is the most accurate as well the fastest and most frugal trading methodology in regard to the current condition of the market and any and all changes within the underlying condition. This means that Zone-trader Philosophy adapts to any and all current trading conditions and the changes within them on the fly, and it does by combining Fibonacci based support and resistance levels with patterns in candlesticks that utilize Fibonacci sequence numbers at the base for the time of each candle on 5 time frames. This means and or proves that a dynamic trading methodology or strategy can only be created through the combination of price supports and resistances, price patterns, and time.

The Zone-Trader opening range is depicted from MR1 to MS1 and the difference between the two is then multiplied by the key Fibonacci ratios (.618), (1.618), and (2.618). These multiples are then added to MR1 to create MR2, MR3, and MR4, and then subtracted from MS1 to create MS2, MS3 and MS4 and then reversed after the passing MR4 and MS4 which are the tails of the first distribution, which means distribution 1 is MR4 to MS4, distribution 2 is MR4 to MR11 and distribution 3 is MS4 to MS11.

MR11 = MR4 – MR3 + MR10

MR10 = MR3 – MR2 + MR9

MR9 = MR2 – MR1 + MR8

MR8 = MR1 – MS1 + MR7

MR7 = MR3 – MR2 + MR6

MR6 = MR5 – MR4 + MR5

MR5 = MR4 – MR3 + MR4

MR4 = MR1 – MS1 X 2.618 + MR1

MR3 = MR1 – MS1 X 1.618 + MR1

MR2 = MR1 –MS1 X .618 + MR1

MR1 EQUALS THE HIGHEST HIGH OF THE OPENING RANGE

MS1 EQUALS THE LOWEST LOW OF THE OPENING RANGE

MS2 = MS1 – (MR1 – MS1 X .618)

MS3 = MS1 – (MR1 – MS1 X 1.618)

MS4 = MS1 – (MR1 – MS1 X 2.618)

MS5 = MS4 – (MS3 – MS4)

MS6 = MS5 – (MS5 – MS4)

MS7 = MS6 – (MS1 – MS2)

MS8 = MS7 – (MR1-MS1)

MS9 = MS8 – (MS1 – MS2)

MS10 = MS9 – (MS2 – MS3)

MS11 = MS10 – (MS3 – MS4)

Each distribution contains is own neutral zone, bullish and bearish breakout zones, bullish and bearish confirmation zones, and bullish and bearish trend extension zones. MR1 to MS1 is the neutral zone, MR1 to MR2 equals the bullish breakout zone, MR2 to MR3 equals the bullish confirmation zone, and MR3 to MR4 equals the bullish trend extension zone. MS1 to MS2 equals the bearish breakout zone,

MS2 to MS3 equals the bearish confirmation zone, MS3 to MS4 equals the bearish trend extension zone. This makes MR4 and MS4 the third deviation from the zone-trader pivot or the point of control (POC) which is the midpoint of the neutral zone.

Distribution 2 equals MR4 to MR11, which makes MR7 to MR8 the neutral zone of distribution 2 and the midpoint between mr7 and mr8 and depicted in royal the midpoint between the 2 is the zone-trader pivot of distribution2 or the point of control (POC) and depicted in white. MR8 to MR9 depicted in cyan is the bullish breakout zone of distribution 2. MR9 to MR10 is depicted in magenta and is the bullish confirmation zone of distribution 2. MR10 to MR11 is depicted in yellow and is the bullish trend extension zone of the distribution 2. MR7 to MR6 is the bearish breakout zone of distribution 2 and is depicted in cyan. MR6 to MR5 is the bearish confirmation of distribution 2 and is depicted in magenta. MR5 to MR4 is the bearish trend extension zone of distribution 2 and is depicted in yellow.

Distribution 3 equals MS4 to MS11, which makes MS7 to MS8 the neutral zone distribution 3 depicted in Royal blue and the midpoint between the zone-trader pivot or the (POC) point of control is depicted in white. MS7 to MS6 is the bullish confirmation zone of distribution 3 and depicted in cyan. MS6 to MS5 is the bullish confirmation zone of distribution 3 and is depicted in magenta. MS5 to MS4 is the bullish trend extension zone of distribution 3 and depicted in yellow. MS8 to MS9 is the bearish breakout zone of distribution 3 and depicted in cyan. MS9 to MS10 is the bearish confirmation zone of distribution 3 and is depicted in magenta. MS10 to MS11 is the bearish trend extension zone of distribution 3 and is depicted in yellow.

The Neutral Zone which is MR1 to MS1 distribution 1, MR7 to MR8 distribution 2, and MS7 to MS8 distribution 3. Each of the 3 neutral zones contain within them what I refer to as the balanced oscillation area this area is denoted from the midpoint between the zone-trader pivot and MR1 to the midpoint between the zone-trader pivot and MS1 in distribution 1, and respectively in distribution 2 and distribution 3 which means the balanced oscillation area in distribution 2 is from the midpoint between the zone-trader pivot of distribution 2 and MR8 to the midpoint between the zone-trader pivot of distribution 2 and MR7, and the balanced oscillation area of distribution 3 is the midpoint between the zone-trader pivot of distribution 3 and ms7 to the midpoint between the zone-trader pivot of distribution 3 and MS8.

The balanced oscillation area is where the market fluctuates back and forth around the POC or the Zone-Trader pivot in a balanced state, which means that fair prices exist and are being agreed upon between the bulls and the bears. In order to breakout of a balanced oscillation state unfair prices will have to be declared by either buyers or sellers in the form of and influx of buy orders from bulls that overpower the sell orders by bears in quantity as well as type as this would normally result from market buys and buy stops which get converted to a market order and filled at the next tick, and or an influx of sells from the bears that overpower the number of buy orders from bulls in quantity and normally in the form of market sells and or sell stops which then get converted to a market order and filled at the next tick. In order for the market to breakout of balanced oscillating state I have determined that a candle body close above the midpoint between the zone-trader pivot and MR1, MR8 or MS7 must occur in the bullish direction in order to attempt to establish a bullish breakout and a candle body close between the zone-trader pivot and MS1, MR7, and MS8 must occur in order for the market to breakout of balanced oscillating state in the bearish direction and attempt to establish a bearish breakout.

If a candle body close is established above the top of the balanced oscillation area or below the bottom of the balanced oscillation area then this footprint is then established in the market and unfair prices can then be declared alerting me the trader to look for pivot bounce which means looking for buy signal if the candle body close is above the top of the balanced oscillation area, which would be denoted by the market retracing down from the top of the balanced oscillation area finding support at the zone-trader pivot and then establishing a candle body close higher than the high of the prior candle, and vice versa if the market is breaking out of the balanced oscillation area in the bearish direction then I the trader would then look for a retracement from the bottom of the balanced oscillation area towards the POC and then for the market to find resistance at the zone-trader pivot and then establish a candle body close lower than the low of the prior candle for a sell signal to occur which again suggest the market will now market and attempt at a bearish breakout and attempt to move into the bearish breakout zone from MS1 to MS2 when then again the fight will resume in order to determine if fair or unfair prices can be agreed upon.

What Is the Opening Range?

Technical analyst utilize what is referred to as the opening range while watching and or trading auction based markets. The opening range is defined as the opening domicile time interval for any auction based market. According to Mark Fisher author The Logical Trader "The opening range is the is the initial time frame of trading for a stock, commodity, currency, bond, or other financial derivatives at the start of each new trading session" (Fisher, P.10). Investopedia defines the opening range as follows, "the opening range (OR) describes a security's high and low price for a short period just after the market opens, often the first fifteen minutes of the trading day" (Investopedia.com).

Also according to Fisher it is the most important price range to auction based market trading and has statistical significance. Fisher says, "Now if I told you that volatile markets not static and not necessarily trending markets the opening range tends to be the high or the low 17 to 23 percent of the time. Because this observation would tell you the opening range being the high or the low 1/5 of the time is what we call statistically significant. In complete layman's terms this means the opening range is not just another 10 minute out of 32 of them in the trading day. It has more weight than any other time interval" (Fisher, P.12).

"The opening range is important for some traders as it can be a period of high volume and volatility that then sets the tone for the rest of the trading day. Indeed, some research points to the fact that a day's high or low being printed during the opening minutes of trading is far more frequent than a random walk would suggest. Day traders often monitor a stock's opening range because it can provide an indication of market sentiment and price trend for the day" (Investopedia.com).

Traders can utilize the opening range for a breakout, trend establishment and or a failure of each look to position themselves for a mean reversion trade. Since all auction based market move the same way they go from a balanced state, then they go into a transitioning state then they go into a trending state then they go back into a transition state and finally back to a balanced state. In other words markets establish an opening range, where fair prices are being agreed upon for a specific defined time range, then the market attempts to breakout of the this range, by either the bulls or the bears declaring unfair prices. If the bulls declare unfair prices then the market will breakout of the opening range to the upside and vice a versa if the bears declare unfair prices the market will break out of the opening range to the downside.

Fisher also states, "there is one other important thing to consider about the opening range, and that is making sure it's based on its domicile market. What do I mean by that if you're trading natural gas futures the you know the domicile market is the New York Mercantile Exchange. That's where the opening range is established. But if you were trading say, Japanese Yen, then the opening of the U.S. currency market wouldn't apply. Rather, you'd have to look to the opening of the Japanese markets" (Fisher, P.11).

This is important to note for the accuracy and significance of the Zone-Trader Philosophy model, since my trading methodology utilizes an opening range created only from Fibonacci number sequence based numerals. The opening time has to be specific in order to calculate my Zone-trader Philosophy Yearly, Quarterly, Monthly, Weekly, and daily profiles. IN order to calculate the daily profiles for commodities or futures contracts the trader will want to use the opening time of the pit as the initial opening time and then calculate the rest of the time interval for the range from there. In order to calculate the daily profile for trading of stocks traders will want to utilize the NYSE opening, and for the Forex markets traders can use 7:30 pm pst for Japenese Yen, and other currencies in that time range. The opening for European markets is 10:30 pm pst this includes the Euro, British Pound, and Swiss Franc. The U.S. dollar the trader can us the opening of the DX or the U.S. dollar index which trades on the Ice exchange. For the Canadian dollar in forex the pit opening of the Canadian dollar futures will suffice. \

The trader will notice that most of the opening times pertain to time zone morning hours in which the vehicle or financial instrument being traded resides within. This where the where the Zone-Trader can identify that key opening volume spike that provides statistical significance, in other words where fair prices are firstly identified on the day and the markets price movement will adhere to this range until either the bulls or the bears declare unfair prices and cause the market to move out of a balanced oscillating state. The midpoint of the Opening range is the Zone-Trader Pivot or the point of the control and the underlying market's price movement will oscillate back forth across the point of control in a fair prices state, until either the bears or the bulls declare unfair prices and break the market out of balanced oscillation.

In order to calculate the Weekly profile the trader must take one full day of trading from the first trading day of the week. This means the start of the first day of trading will be the pre-determined opening time that is used for the calculation of the daily profile until the close of the specific underlying financial instrument of that same day, for the first trading day of the week. Then the trader will consider that high to the low of the specifically pre-determined daily trading range as the opening range for the week.

The calculation for the Monthly Profile the trader must the entire price range for the first entire week of the month's trading, In other words the highest high and the lowest low of the first week of the month, which primarily will be 5 trading days but due to holidays sometimes it can be 3, or 4 trading days.

The calculation for the Quarterly Profile the trader must use the first x-amount of days of the quarter depending on the underlying financial instrument entire range. In other words the highest high minus the lowest low for the first 8, 13, and or 21 days of the Quarter. This entire range is the opening range of the Quarter and resets every 3 months, meaning the first x-amount of days in January calculates the first Quarters opening range. The second quarter's opening range is calculated using the first x-amount of days in the month of April.

The Third quarter’s opening range is calculated using the first x-amount of days in the month of July and the fourth quarter’s opening range is calculated using the first x-amount of days in the month of October.

The Yearly Profile is calculated by taking the first 8, 13, or 21 weeks of the year, again depending on the underlying financial instrument being traded.

The opening range is computed on all 5 profiles for each of the sectors within the commodities, stock, ETF's and forex markets.

THE ZONE-TRADER CALCULATION FORMULA

The sectors I primarily trade are Financials, Metals, Grains, Currencies, and oil and gases. The opening ranges for financials including stocks and ETF's, metals and grains are 13 weeks, 13 days, 5 days, 1 day, 13 minutes. The opening ranges for Currencies 21 weeks, 21 days, 5 days, 1 day, 21 minutes. The opening ranges for Oil and gases are 8 weeks 8 days, 5 days, 1 day, 8 minutes. Zone-Trader™ is a predefined market arena for trading auction based markets that seeks to capture the current psychology of underlying market on multiple time frames in order to determine or predict future market direction. Zone-Trader™ employs three distributions per profile and currently five profiles. The profiles are Yearly, Quarterly, Monthly, Weekly and Daily.

Each Distribution contains the same seven predefined and specifically labeled zones. These are: (Neutral Zone, Bullish Breakout Zone, Bullish Confirmation Zone, Bullish Trend Extension Zone, Bearish Breakout Zone, Bearish Confirmation Zone and Bearish Trend Extension Zone) we use these to order, profile and interpret condition of market to provide traders a specific description of where the market is and what it is trying to do.Zone-Trader™ is a newly created, intuitive form of auction market theory by Matthew D. Reynolds.

I Matthew Dwyer Reynolds the creator of Zone-Trader Philosophy understood that auction markets primarily move within three conditions: balanced, trending or transitioning. Zone-Trader™ utilizes these three conditions to incorporate them into its predefined market arena through the definition and labeling of its trading zones.

Auction based markets all do the same thing. For example, they breakout, they establish trend or they extend the trend. If they cannot breakout, they reverse to the point of control. If they cannot establish a trend, they reverse to the point of control. If they cannot extend the trend, they reverse to the point of control. Through his auction market trading knowledge, wisdom and intuition, Mr. Reynolds uses these conditions and normal market movements to create the ability to capture the current psychology of the market by defining the zones and labeling them either Bullish or Bearish. The midpoint of the Neutral Zone is the Zone-Trader™ Pivot --point of control.

Zones above the Neutral Zone are Bullish Zones. Zones below the Neutral Zone are Bearish Zones. The order of the Bullish and Bearish Zones are identical and specifically labeled in this manner to capture the specific condition or movement of the current market trend (Breakout, Trend Confirmation or Trend Extension). Each zone contains a specific rule that is used to determine or predict the future underlying market direction. Whether specific condition as described by each zone rule is achieved or not creates the ability to capture market psychology upon that profile or time frame and generates buy or sell signals accordingly. There are a total of 36 rules, 12 rules per distribution. Our separate Rules Document pictorially describes each specific rule with specific detail aligned with description to enhance clarity and understanding for the trader. The combination of 5 profiles looking at long-term to short-term perspective and understanding that Long-Term overpowers Short-Term provides the ability to create strategies.

The Zone-Trader opening range is depicted from MR1 to MS1 and the difference between the two is then multiplied by the key Fibonacci ratios (.618), (1.618), and (2.618). These multiples are then added to MR1 to create MR2, MR3, and MR4, and then subtracted from MS1 to create MS2, MS3 and MS4 and then reversed after the passing MR4 and MS4 which are the tails of the first distribution, which means distribution 1 is MR4 to MS4, distribution 2 is MR4 to MR11 and distribution 3 is MS4 to MS11.

Each distribution contains is own neutral zone, bullish and bearish breakout zones, bullish and bearish confirmation zones, and bullish and bearish trend extension zones. MR1 to MS1 is the neutral zone, MR1 to MR2 equals the bullish breakout zone, MR2 to MR3 equals the bullish confirmation zone, and MR3 to MR4 equals the bullish trend extension zone. MS1 to MS2 equals the bearish breakout zone, MS2 to MS3 equals the bearish confirmation zone, MS3 to MS4 equals the bearish trend extension zone. This makes MR4 and MS4 the third deviation from the zone-trader pivot or the point of control (POC) which is the midpoint of the neutral zone.

Distribution 2 equals MR4 to MR11, which makes MR7 to MR8 the neutral zone of distribution 2 and the midpoint between mr7 and mr8 and depicted in royal the midpoint between the 2 is the zone-trader pivot of distribution2 or the point of control (POC) and depicted in white. MR8 to MR9 depicted in cyan is the bullish breakout zone of distribution 2. MR9 to MR10 is depicted in magenta and is the bullish confirmation zone of distribution 2. MR10 to MR11 is depicted in yellow and is the bullish trend extension zone of the distribution 2. MR7 to MR6 is the bearish breakout zone of distribution 2 and is depicted in cyan. MR6 to MR5 is the bearish confirmation of distribution 2 and is depicted in magenta. MR5 to MR4 is the bearish trend extension zone of distribution 2 and is depicted in yellow.

Distribution 3 equals MS4 to MS11, which makes MS7 to MS8 the neutral zone distribution 3 depicted in Royal blue and the midpoint between then the zone-trader pivot or the (POC) point of control is depicted in white. MS7 to MS6 is the bullish confirmation zone of distribution 3 and depicted in cyan. MS6 to MS5 is the bullish confirmation zone of distribution 3 and is depicted in magenta. MS5 to MS4 is the bullish trend extension zone of distribution 3 and depicted in yellow. MS8 to MS9 is the bearish breakout zone of distribution 3 and depicted in cyan. MS9 to MS10 is the bearish confirmation zone of distribution 3 and is depicted in magenta. MS10 to MS11 is the bearish trend extension zone of distribution 3 and is depicted in yellow.

The Neutral Zone which is MR1 to MS1 distribution 1, MR7 to MR8 distribution 2, and MS7 to MS8 distribution 3. Each of the 3 neutral zones contain within them what I refer to as the balanced oscillation area this area is denoted from the midpoint between the zone-trader pivot and MR1 to the midpoint between the zone-trader pivot and MS1 in distribution 1, and respectively in distribution 2 and distribution 3 which means the balanced oscillation area in distribution 2 is from the midpoint between the zone-trader pivot of distribution 2 and MR8 to the midpoint between the zone-trader pivot of distribution 2 and MR7, and the balanced oscillation area of distribution 3 is the midpoint between the zone-trader pivot of distribution 3 and ms7 to the midpoint between the zone-trader pivot of distribution 3 and MS8.

The balanced oscillation area is where the market fluctuates back and forth around the POC or the Zone-Trader pivot in a balanced state, which means that fair prices exist and are being agreed upon between the bulls and the bears. In order to breakout of a balanced oscillation state unfair prices will have to be declared by either buyers or sellers in the form of and influx of buy orders from bulls that overpower the sell orders by bears in quantity as well as type as this would normally result from market buys and buy stops which get converted to a market order and filled at the next tick, and or an influx of sells from the bears that overpower the number of buy orders from bulls in quantity and normally in the form of market sells and or sell stops which then get converted to a market order and filled at the next tick. In order for the market to breakout of balanced oscillating state I have determined that a candle body close above the midpoint between the zone-trader pivot and MR1, MR8 or MS7 must occur in the bullish direction in order to attempt to establish a bullish breakout and a candle body close between the zone-trader pivot and MS1, MR7, and MS8 must occur in order for the market to breakout of balanced oscillating state in the bearish direction and attempt to establish a bearish breakout.

If a candle body close is established above the top of the balanced oscillation area or below the bottom of the balanced oscillation area then this footprint is then established in the market and unfair prices can then be declared alerting me the trader to look for pivot bounce which means looking for buy signal if the candle body close is above the top of the balanced oscillation area, which would be denoted by the market retracing down from the top of the balanced oscillation area finding support at the zone-trader pivot and then establishing a candle body close higher than the high of the prior candle, and vice versa if the market is breaking out of the balanced oscillation area in the bearish direction then I the trader would then look for a retracement from the bottom of the balanced oscillation area towards the POC and then for the market to find resistance at the zone-trader pivot and then establish a candle body close lower than the low of the prior candle for a sell signal to occur which again suggest the market will now market and attempt at a bearish breakout and attempt to move into the bearish breakout zone from MS1 to MS2 when then again the fight will resume in order to determine if fair or unfair prices can be agreed upon.

Through my Matthew Dwyer Reynolds wisdom and intuition and knowledge of auction market trading, I was able to use these conditions and normal market movements to create the ability to capture the current psychology of the market by defining the zones and labeling them either Bullish or Bearish. The midpoint of the Neutral Zone is the Zone-Trader™ Pivot -- point of control.

Zones above the Neutral Zone are Bullish Zones. Zones below the Neutral Zone are Bearish Zones. The order of the Bullish and Bearish Zones are identical and specifically labeled in this manner to capture the specific condition or movement of the current market trend (Breakout, Trend Confirmation or Trend Extension).

Each zone contains a specific rule that is used to determine or predict the future underlying market direction. Whether specific condition as described by each zone rule is achieved or not creates the ability to capture market psychology upon that profile or time frame and generates buy or sell signals accordingly.

There are a total of 36 rules, 12 rules per distribution. Our separate Rules Document pictorially describes each specific rule with specific detail aligned with description to enhance clarity and understanding for the trader.

The combination of 5 profiles looking at long-term to short-term perspective and understanding that Long-Term overpowers Short-Term provides the ability to create strategies.

The 36 rules provide traders with what the ZoneTrader™ defines as Directional Bias -- whether to expect prices to decrease and sell or to expect prices to increase and buy. The ZoneTrader™ also utilizes a Control Bias which is derived from the Persistence Zone. So, not only does ZoneTrader™ provide the trader with specific future direction of prices; it also provides traders with the ability to determine who has control of the market -- whether it is the bulls or bears.

Again, Long-Term overpowers short-term, so, it is important to identify who has control of the market on each profile or time frame. It is also important to understand that the longer the time frame, the stronger the Directional and Control Bias. The Persistence Zone Document goes into complete detail upon the description, use of, and theory as it applies to the Persistence Zone or PZ for short.

ZONETRADER TRADING RULES

Rule # 1: **Bullish Breakout Zone (MR1 – MR2)**

When the price is on an uptrend and the candle body closes above the midpoint of MR1 &

MR2 we are in a bullish breakout and look to place a buy order at the first retracement.

We need to see at least 2 candles close lower then the low of the prior candle for a true

Retracement. Then look for a candle body close higher then the high of the prior candle

To generate the buy signal.

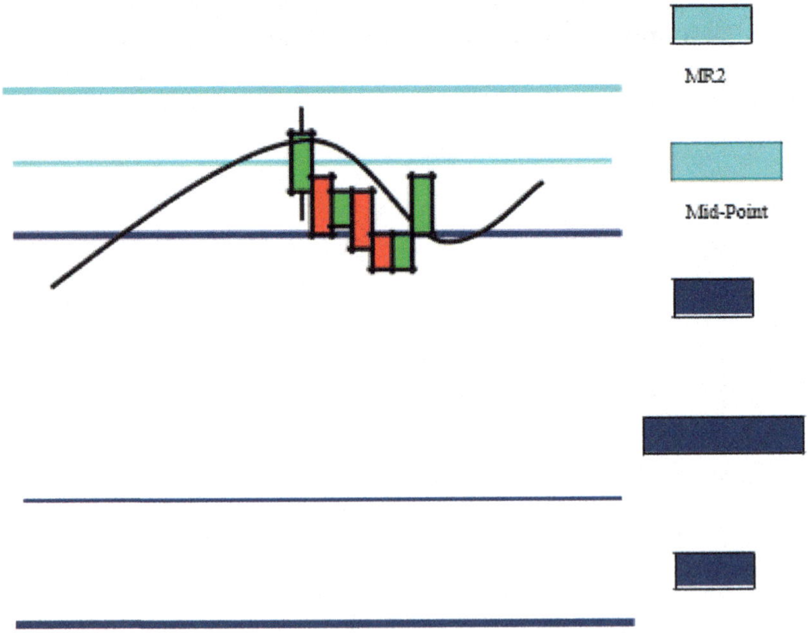

Rule # 2: Failed Bullish Breakout (MR1 – MR2)

When the price is on an uptrend and the candle body fails to close above the midpoint of MR1 & MR2 and then a candle closes lower then the low of the prior candle. We are in a failed bullish breakout and expect the prices to move back to the point of control. Look to sell 1 tick below the low of the prior candle.

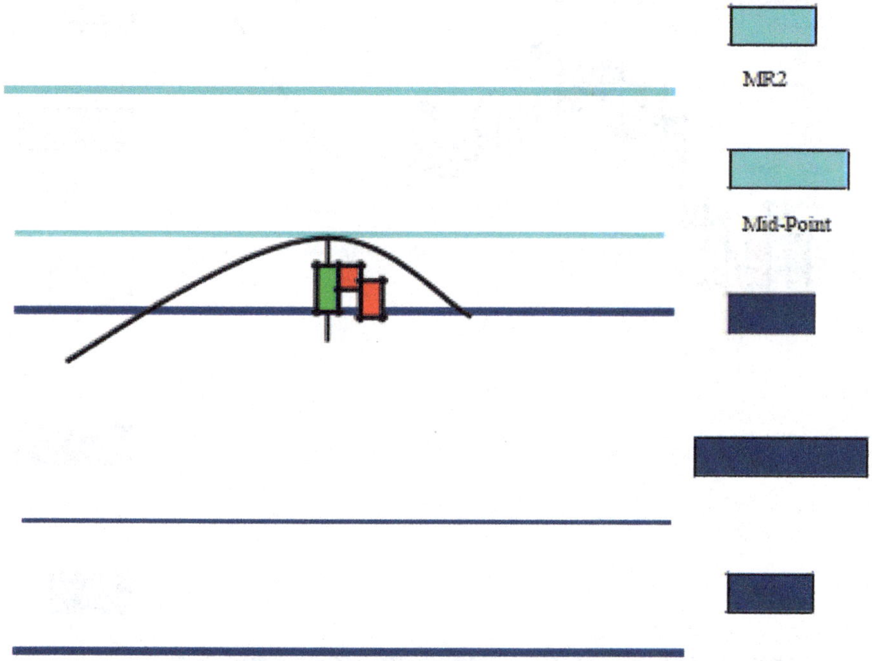

Rule # 3: **Bullish Confirmation Zone (MR2 – MR3)**

If the price stays above MR2 for a specific amount of time (time filter) then a confirmed uptrend is established and we look to buy at the first retracement. Look for 2 closes lower Then the low of the prior candle to be true retrace. Then look for close higher then the high of the prior candle to generate the signal.

Rule # 4: Failed Bullish Confirmation (MR2 – MR3)

If the price breaks above MR2 and fails to hold above MR2 for a specified amount of time (time filter) and then a candle closes lower then the low of the prior candle it indicates failed bullish confirmation of an uptrend and we look to sell and for the prices to trend back towards the point of contol or ZoneTrader Pivot.

Rule # 5: **Bullish Trend Extension Zone (MR3 – MR4)**

If the candle body closes above the midpoint of MR3 & MR4, it indicates the start of trend extension and we look to buy at the first retracement.

Rule # 6: **Failed Bullish Trend Extension (MR3 – MR4)**

If the candle body fails to close above the midpoint of MR3 & MR4, and then a candle closes lower then the low of the prior candle it indicates a failed trend extension and we expect the prices to revert towards the point of control. We sell off the low of the prior candle once we get a close lower than the low of the prior candle.

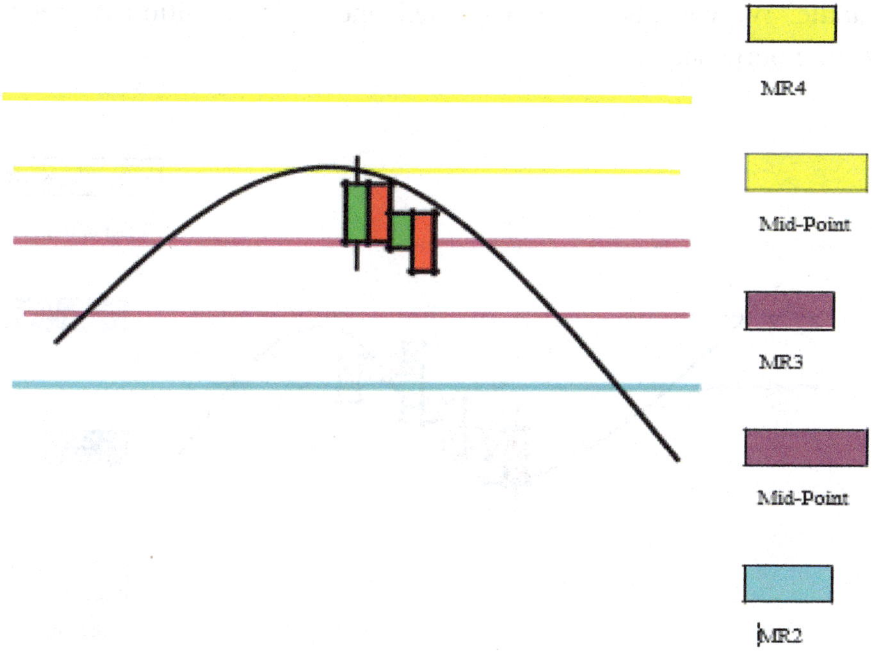

<u>Rule # 7</u>: Bearish Breakout Zone (MS1 – MS2)

When the price is on a downtrend and the candle body closes below the midpoint of MS1 & MS2 we are in a bearish breakout and look to place a sell order at the first retracement. Need to see 2 candles close higher then the high of the prior candle for true retracement. Then a candle has to close lower then the low of the prior candle to generate the sell signal. Sell limit 1 tick below the low of the prior candle. We can also try market sell once this condition is met for testing purposes.

Rule # 8: **Failed Bearish Breakout (MS1 – MS2)**

When the price is on a downtrend and the candle body fails to close below the midpoint of MS1 & MS2 and then a candle closes above the high of the prior candle we are in a failed bearish breakout and look to buy 1 tick above the high of the prior candle and we expect the prices to move back to the point of control or ZoneTrader Pivot.

Rule # 9: Bearish Confirmation Zone (MS2 – MS3)

If the price stays below MS2 for a specific amount of time (time filter) then the market has established or confirmed a downtrend. Look to sell at the first retracement waiting for at least 2 candle closes higher then the high of the prior candle. Once retracement criteria is achieved then look for the first candle to close lower then the low of the prior candle to generate the sell signal. Sell limit 1 tick below the low of the prior candle or at the market for testing purposes.

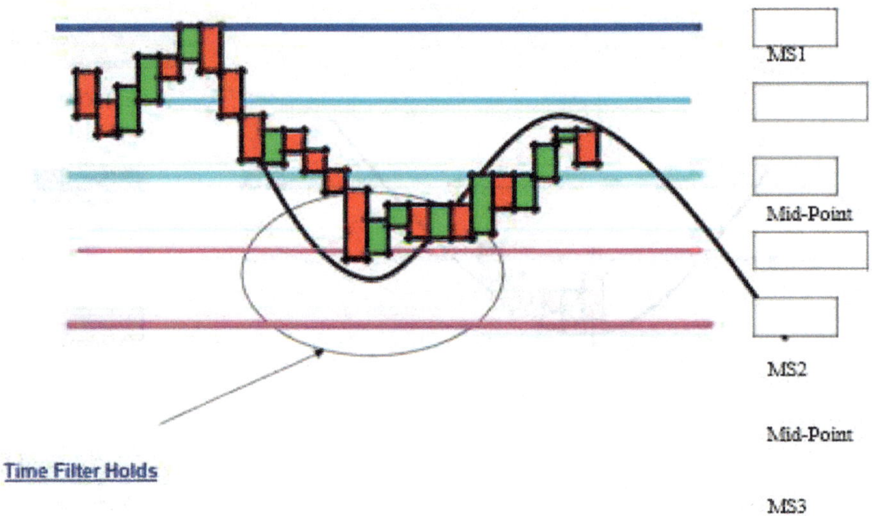

Rule # 10: **Failed Bearish Confirmation (MS2 – MS3)**

If the price fails to hold the time filter below MS2 for a specified amount of time (time filter) and then a candle closes higher then the high of the prior candle this indicates a failed confirmation of a downtrend and we to buy limit 1 tick above the high of the prior candle or at the market for testing purposes. Then we look for the prices to trend back towards the point of control or ZoneTrader Pivot.

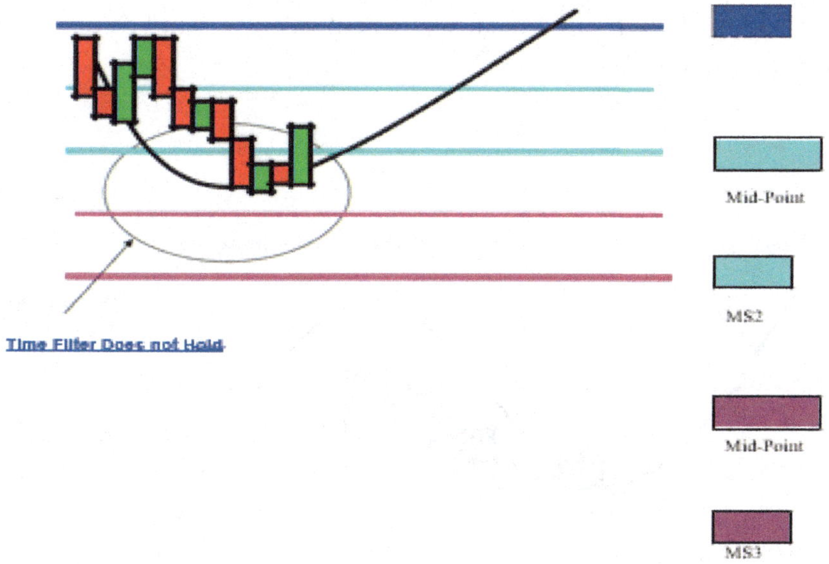

Rule # 11: Bearish Trend Extension Zone (MS3 – MS4)

If the candle body closes below the midpoint of MS3 & MS4, it indicates the market has extended the trend and will attempt to break below MS4 on the next wave down. Look to sell the 1st retracement after the close below the midpoint. Need to see 2 candles close higher then the high of the prior candle for true retracement. Then need to see a candle close lower then the low of the prior candle to generate the sell signal. The reason for this is this suggest the trend is shifting back to the downside, which is what we expect, we just want to make sure that it does before we sell.

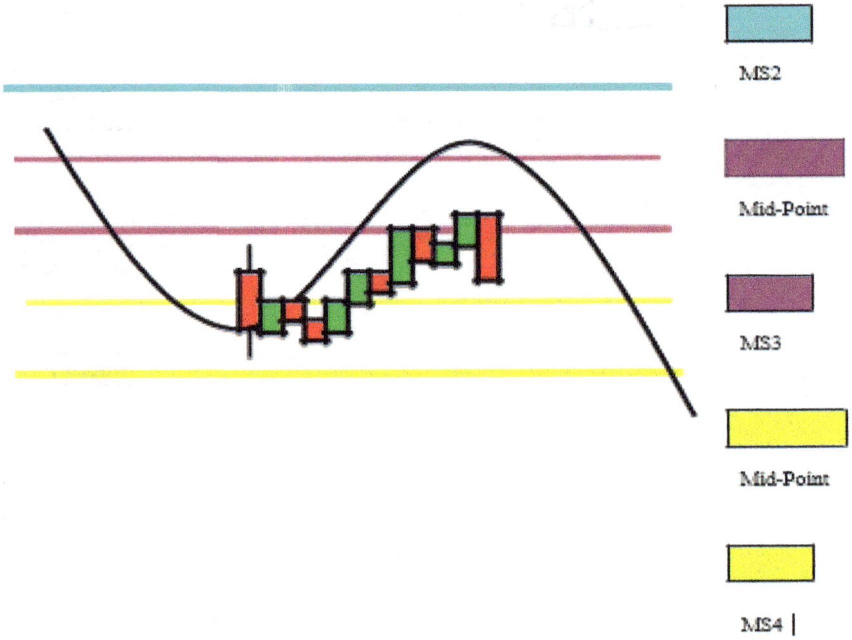

Rule # 12: **Failed Bearish Trend Extension (MS3 – MS4)**

If the candle body fails to close below the midpoint of MS3 & MS4, and then a candle closes higher then the high of the prior candle this indicates a failed bearish trend extension and we look to buy limit 1 tick above the high of the prior candle or at the market for testing purposes. Then we expect the prices to revert towards the point of control or ZoneTrader Pivot.

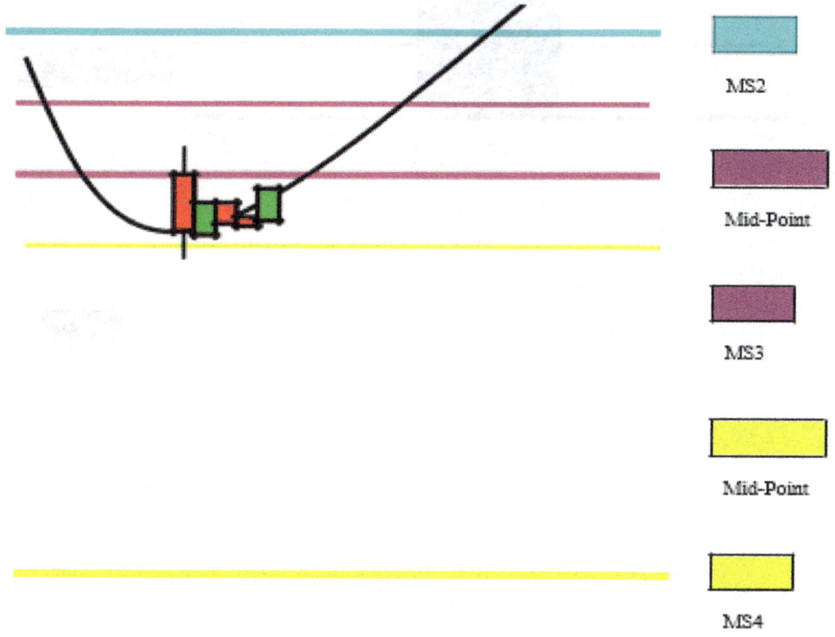

Distributions

1) **Neutral Zone : (MR1 – MS1; Neutral Zone)**

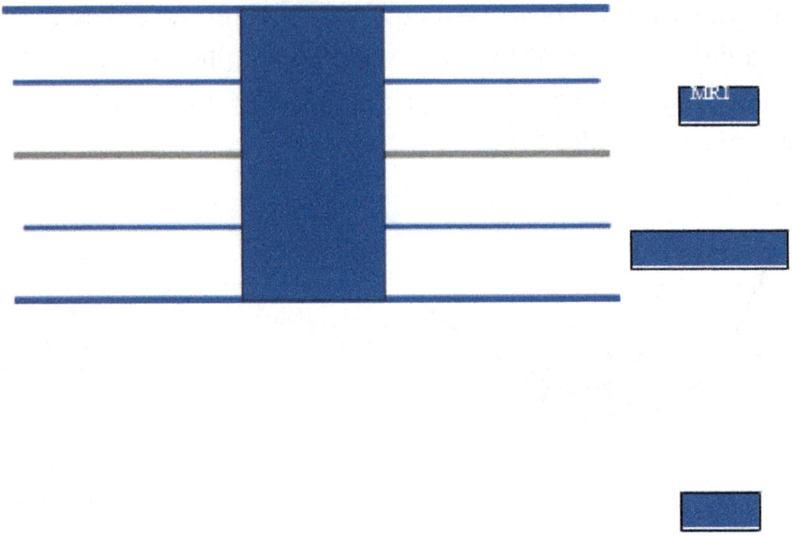

2) Distribution 1: (MR4 – MS4)

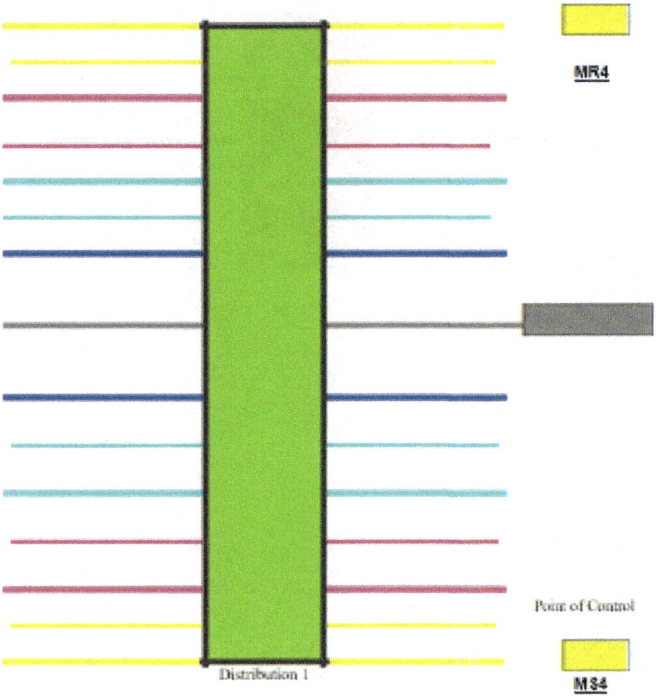

3) Distribution 2: (MR4 – MR11)

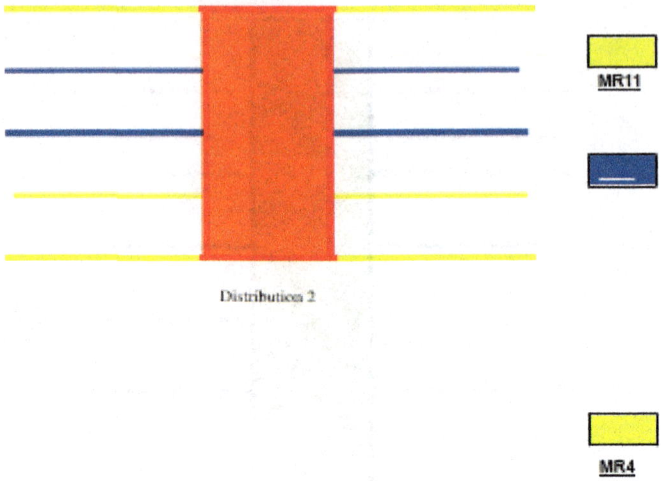

Distribution 2

4) Distribution 3: (MS4 – MS11)

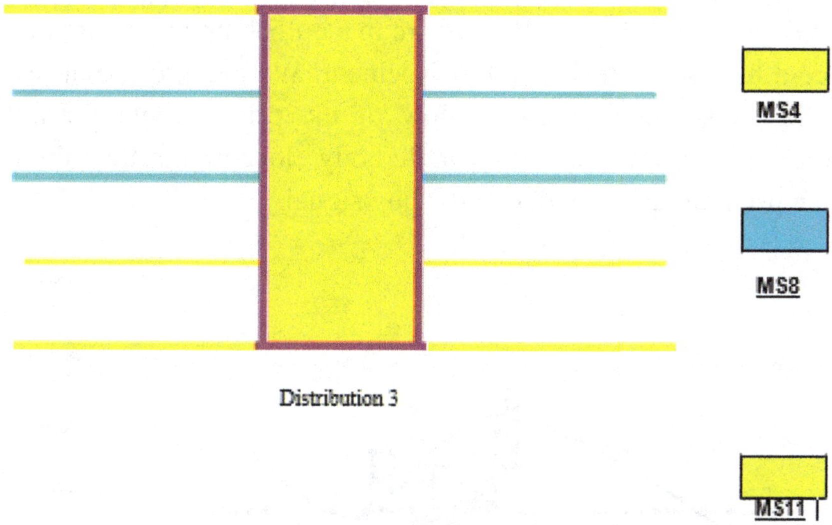

Distribution 3

Rule # 13: **Bullish Breakout Zone; Distribution 2 (MR8 – MR9)**

When the price is on an uptrend and the candle body closes above the midpoint of MR8 & MR9 we are in a bullish breakout and look to place a buy order at the first retracement. We need to see at least 2 candles close lower then the low of the prior candle for a true retracement. Then look for a candle body close higher then the high of the prior candle to generate the buy signal.

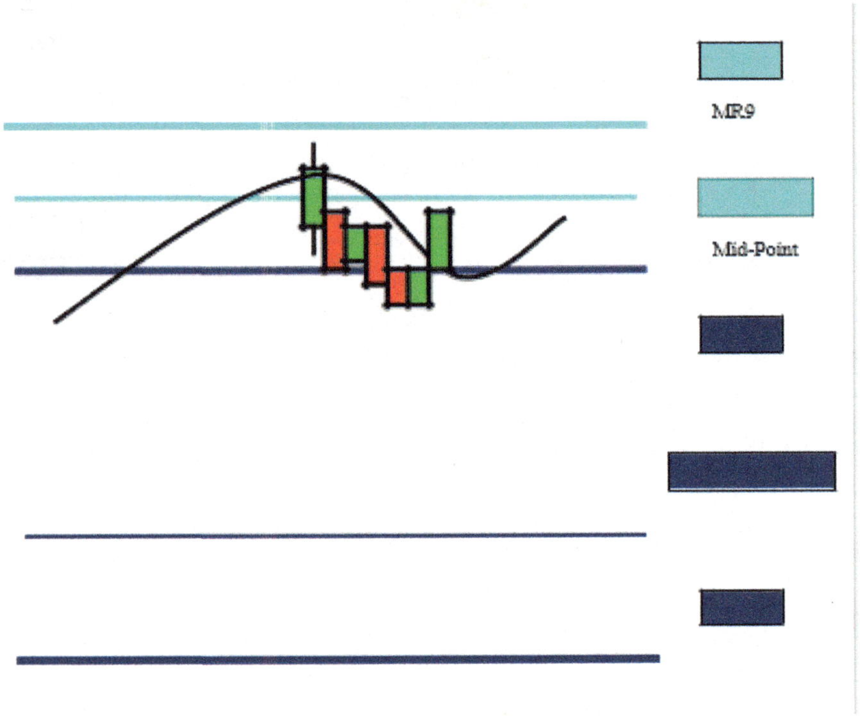

Rule # 14: **Failed Bullish Breakout; Distribution 2 (MR8 – MR9)**

When the price is on an uptrend and the candle body fails to close above the midpoint of MR8 & MR9 and then a candle closes lower then the low of the prior candle. We are in a failed bullish breakout and expect the prices to move back to the point of control. Look to sell 1 tick below the low of the prior candle.

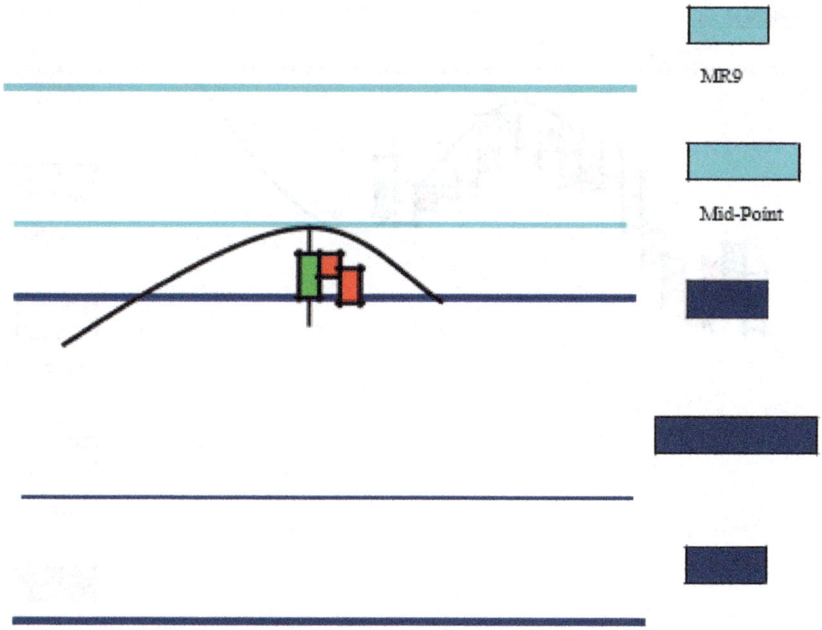

Rule # 15: **Bullish Confirmation Zone; Distribution 2 (MR9 – MR10)**

If the price stays above MR9 for a specific amount of time (time filter) then a confirmed uptrend is established and we look to buy at the first retracement. Look for 2 closes lower Then the low of the prior candle to be true retrace. Then look for close higher then the high of the prior candle to generate the signal.

<u>Rule # 16</u>: Failed Bullish Confirmation; Distribution 2 (MR9 – MR10)

If the price breaks above MR9 and fails to hold above MR10 for a specified amount of time (time filter) and then a candle closes lower then the low of the prior candle it indicates failed bullish confirmation of an uptrend and we look to sell and for the prices to trend back towards the point of contol or ZoneTrader Pivot.

<u>Rule # 17</u>: Bullish Trend Extension Zone; Distribution 2 (MR10 – MR11)

If the candle body closes above the midpoint of MR10 & MR11, it indicates the start of trend extension and we look to buy at the first retracement.

Rule # 18: **Failed Bullish Trend Extension; Distribution 2 (MR10 – MR11)**

If the candle body fails to close above the midpoint of MR10 & MR11, and then a candle closes lower then the low of the prior candle it indicates a failed trend extension and we expect the prices to revert towards the point of control.

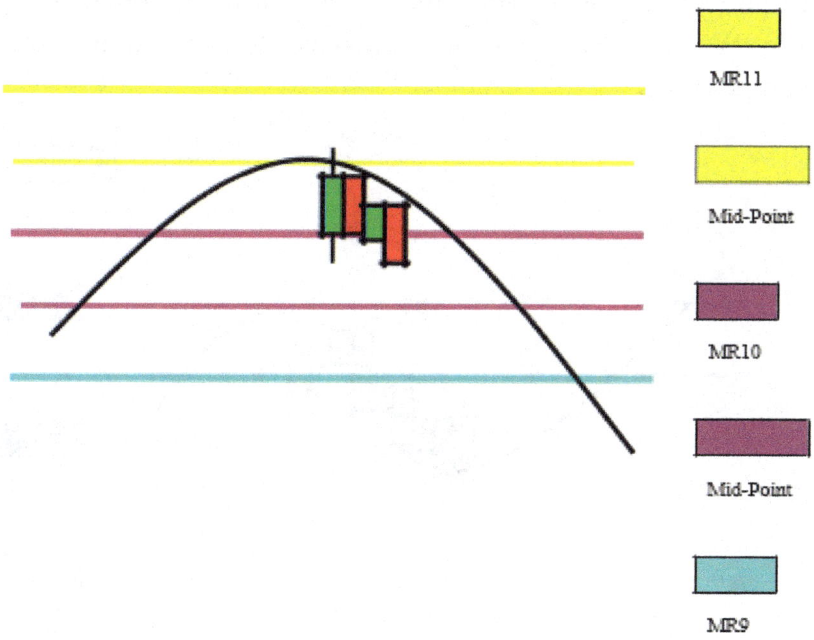

Rule # 19: Bearish Breakout Zone; Distribution 2 (MR6 – MR7)

When the price is on a downtrend and the candle body closes below the midpoint of MR6 & MR7 we are in a bearish breakout and look to place a sell order at the first retracement. Need to see 2 candles close higher then the high of the prior candle for true retracement. Then a candle has to close lower then the low of the prior candle to generate the sell signal. Sell limit 1 tick below the low of the prior candle. We can also try market sell once this condition is met for testing purposes.

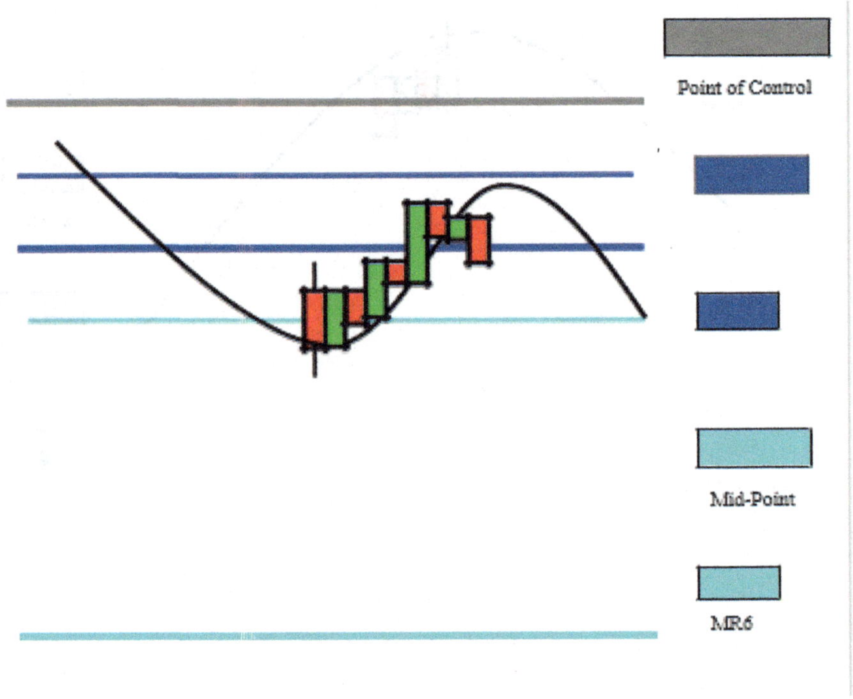

Rule # 20: Failed Bearish Breakout; Distribution 2 (MR6 – MR7)

When the price is on a downtrend and the candle body fails to close below the midpoint of MR6 & MR7 and then a candle closes above the high of the prior candle we are in a failed bearish breakout and look to buy 1 tick above the high of the prior candle and we expect the prices to move back to the point of control or ZoneTrader Pivot.

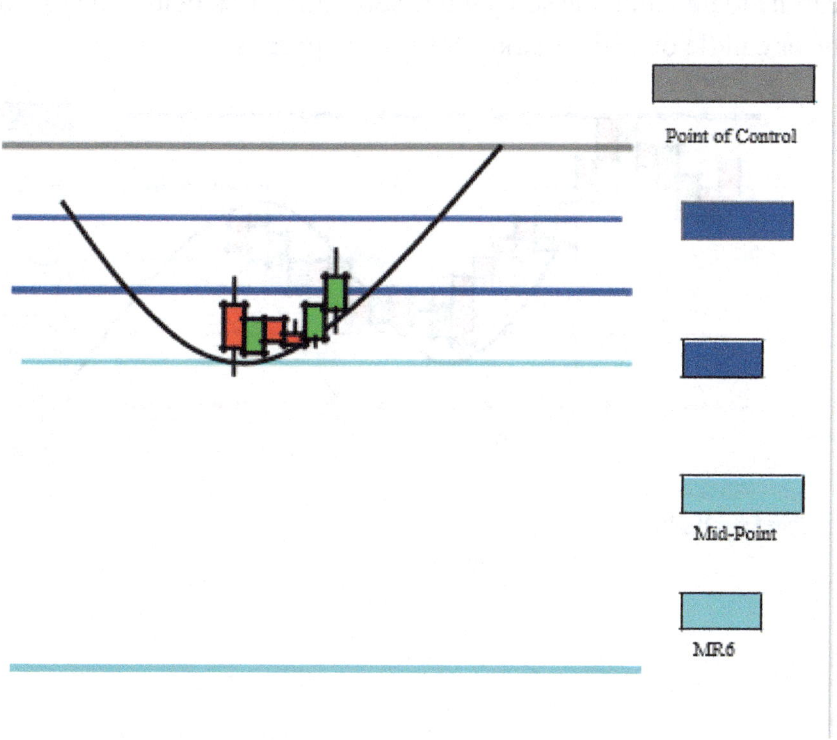

Rule # 21: **Bearish Confirmation Zone; Distribution 2 (MR5 – MR6)**

If the price stays below MR5 for a specific amount of time (time filter) then the market has established or confirmed a downtrend. Look to sell at the first retracement waiting for at least 2 candle closes higher then the high of the prior candle. Once retracement criteria is achieved then look for the first candle to close lower then the low of the prior candle to generate the sell signal. Sell limit 1 tick below the low of the prior candle or at the market for testing purposes.

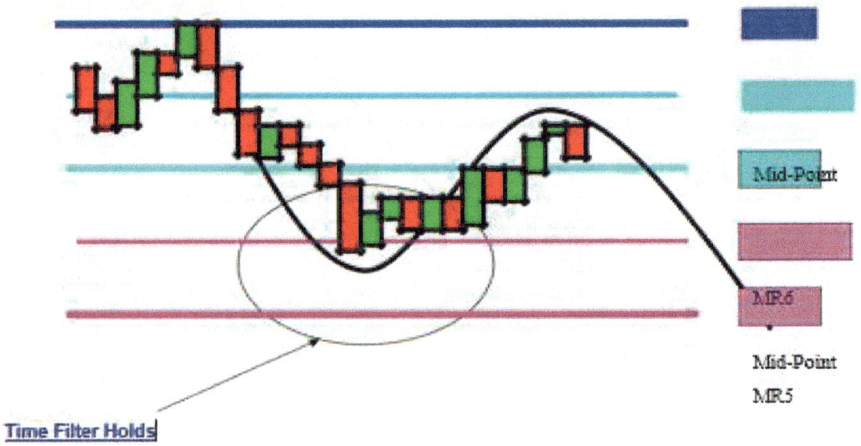

Rule # 22: Failed Bearish Confirmation; Distribution 2 (MR5 – MR6)

If the price fails to hold the time filter below MR5 for a specified amount of time (time filter) and then a candle closes higher then the high of the prior candle this indicates a failed confirmation of a downtrend and we to buy limit 1 tick above the high of the prior candle or at the market for testing purposes. Then we look for the prices to trend back towards the point of control or ZoneTrader Pivot.

Rule # 23: **Bearish Trend Extension Zone; Distribution 2 (MR4 – MR5)**

If the candle body closes below the midpoint of MR4 & MR5, it indicates the market has extended the trend and will attempt to break below MR4 on the next wave down. Look to sell the 1st retracement after the close below the midpoint. Need to see 2 candles close higher then the high of the prior candle for true retracement. Then need to see a candle close lower then the low of the prior candle to generate the sell signal. The reason for this is this suggest the trend is shifting back to the downside, which is what we expect, we just want to make sure that it does before we sell.

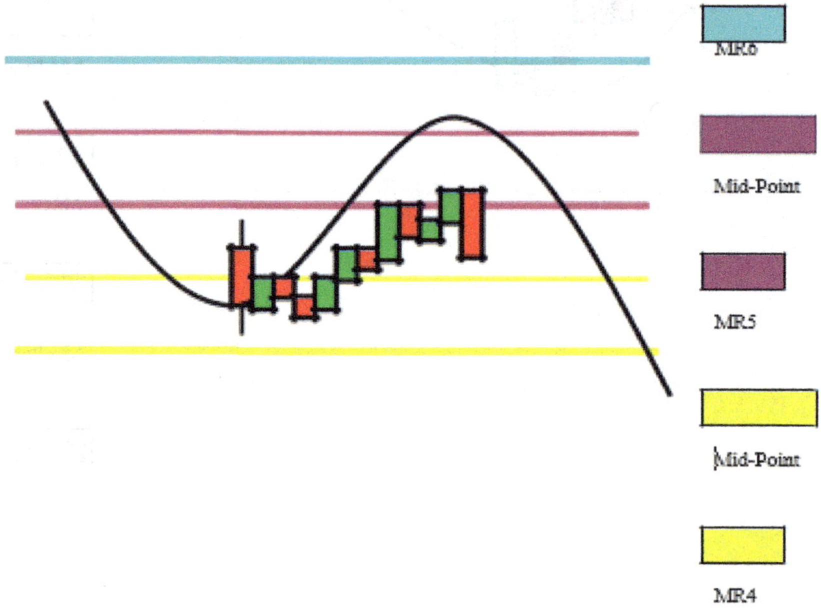

Rule # 24: **Failed Bearish Trend Extension; Distribution 2 (MR4 – MR5)**

If the candle body fails to close below the midpoint of MR4 & MR5, and then a candle closes higher then the high of the prior candle this indicates a failed bearish trend extension and we look to buy limit 1 tick above the high of the prior candle or at the market for testing purposes. Then we expect the prices to revert towards the point of control or ZoneTrader Pivot.

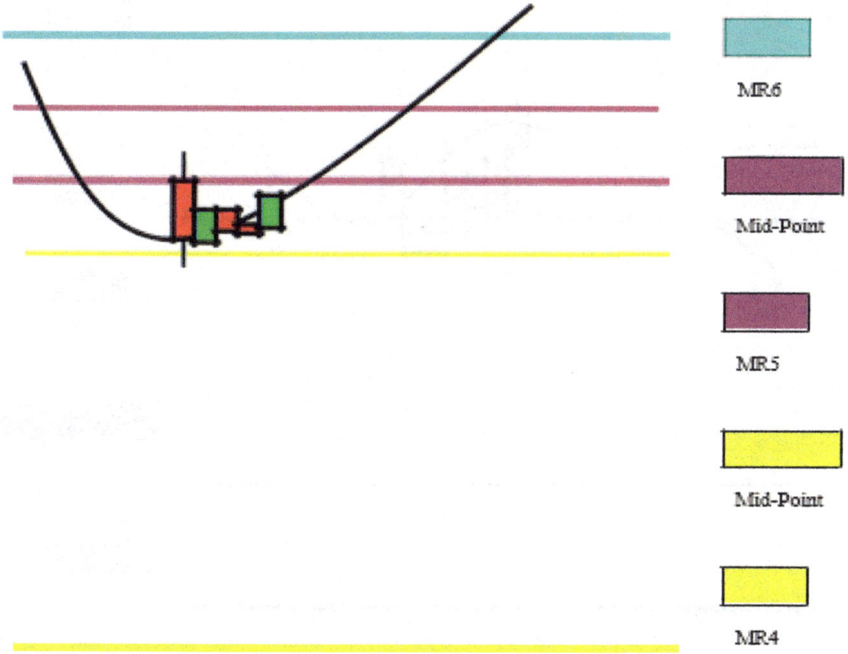

Rule # 25: Bullish Breakout Zone; Distribution 3 (MS7 – MS6)

When the price is on an uptrend and the candle body closes above the midpoint of MS8 & MS9 we are in a bullish breakout and look to place a buy order at the first retracement. We need to see at least 2 candles close lower then the low of the prior candle for a true retracement. Then look for a candle body close higher then the high of the prior candle to generate the buy signal.

Rule # 26: Failed Bullish Breakout; Distribution 3 (MS7 – MS6)

When the price is on an uptrend and the candle body fails to close above the midpoint of MS8 & MS9 and then a candle closes lower then the low of the prior candle. We are in a failed bullish breakout and expect the prices to move back to the point of control. Look to sell 1 tick below the low of the prior candle.

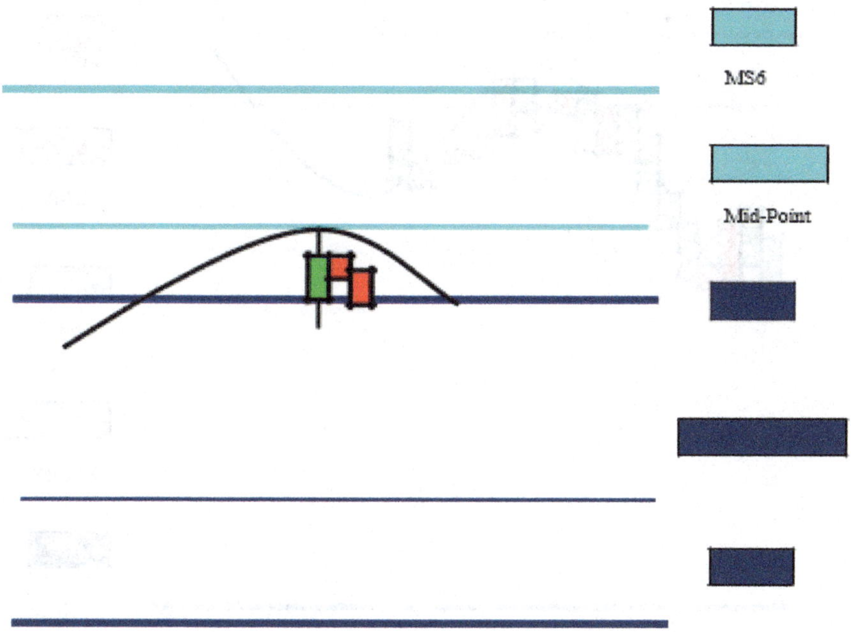

Rule # 27: Bullish Confirmation Zone; Distribution 3 (MS6 – MS5)

If the price stays above MS9 for a specific amount of time (time filter) then a confirmed uptrend is established and we look to buy at the first retracement. Look for 2 closes lower Then the low of the prior candle to be true retrace. Then look for close higher then the high of the prior candle to generate the signal.

Rule # 28: **Failed Bullish Confirmation; Distribution 3 (MS6 – MS5)**

If the price breaks above MS9 and fails to hold above MS10 for a specified amount of time (time filter) and then a candle closes lower then the low of the prior candle it indicates failed bullish confirmation of an uptrend and we look to sell and for the prices to trend back towards the point of contol or ZoneTrader Pivot.

Rule # 29: **Bullish Trend Extension Zone; Distribution 3 (MS4 – MS5)**

If the candle body closes above the midpoint of MS10 & MS11, it indicates the start of trend extension and we look to buy at the first retracement.

Rule # 30: Failed Bullish Trend Extension; Distribution 3 (MS4 – MS5)

If the candle body fails to close above the midpoint of MR10 & MR11, and then a candle closes lower then the low of the prior candle it indicates a failed trend extension and we expect the prices to revert towards the point of control.

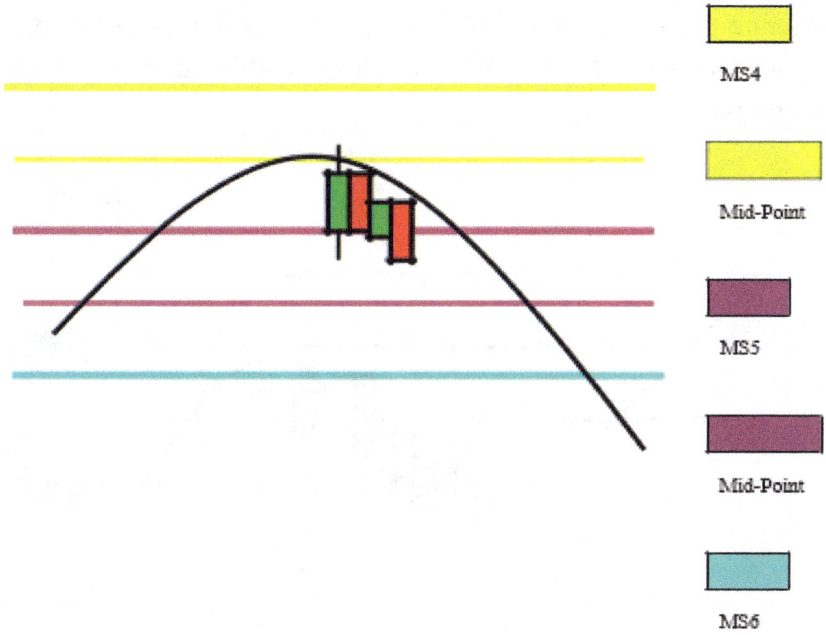

<u>Rule # 31</u>: Bearish Breakout Zone; Distribution 3 (MS8 – MS9)

When the price is on a downtrend and the candle body closes below the midpoint of MS6 & MS7 we are in a bearish breakout and look to place a sell order at the first retracement. Need to see 2 candles close higher then the high of the prior candle for true retracement. Then a candle has to close lower then the low of the prior candle to generate the sell signal. Sell limit 1 tick below the low of the prior candle. We can also try market sell once this condition is met for testing purposes.

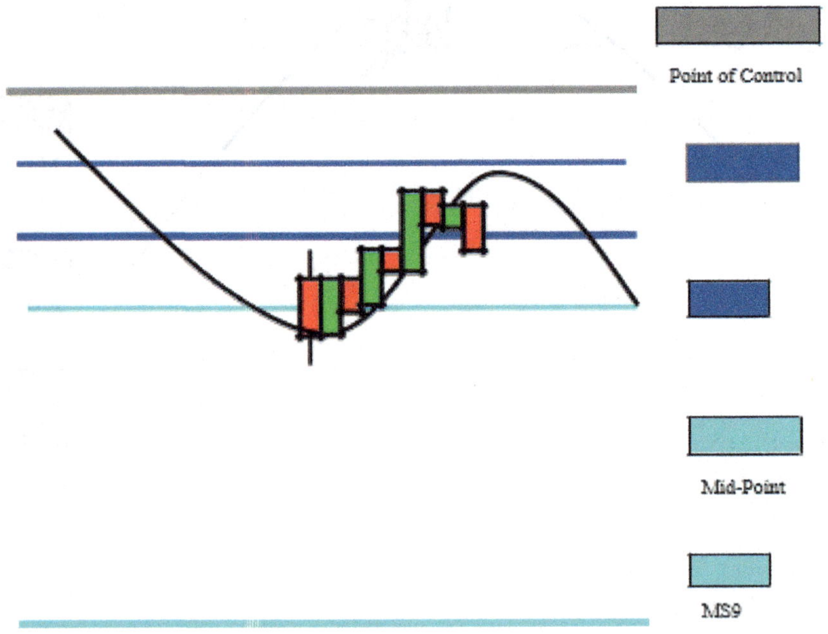

Rule # 32: Failed Bearish Breakout; Distribution 3 (MS8 – MS9)

When the price is on a downtrend and the candle body fails to close below the midpoint of MS6 & MS7 and then a candle closes above the high of the prior candle we are in a failed bearish breakout and look to buy 1 tick above the high of the prior candle and we expect the prices to move back to the point of control or ZoneTrader Pivot.

<u>Rule # 33</u>: **Bearish Confirmation Zone; Distribution 3 (MS9 – MS10)**

If the price stays below MS5 for a specific amount of time (time filter) then the market has established or confirmed a downtrend. Look to sell at the first retracement waiting for

At least 2 candle closes higher then the high of the prior candle. Once retracement criteria is achieved then look for the first candle to close lower then the low of the prior candle to generate the sell signal. Sell limit 1 tick below the low of the prior candle or at the market for testing purposes.

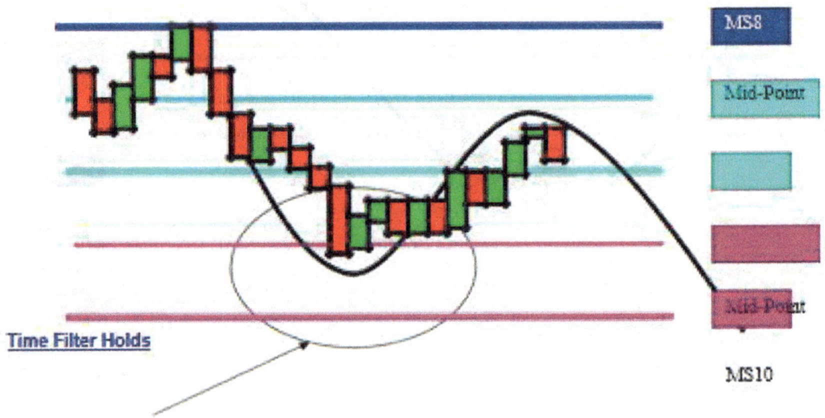

Rule # 34: **Failed Bearish Confirmation; Distribution 3 (MS9 – MS10)**

If the price fails to hold the time filter below MS5 for a specified amount of time (time filter) and then a candle closes higher then the high of the prior candle this indicates a failed confirmation of a downtrend and we to buy limit 1 tick above the high of the prior candle or at the market for testing purposes. Then we look for the prices to trend back towards the point of control or ZoneTrader Pivot.

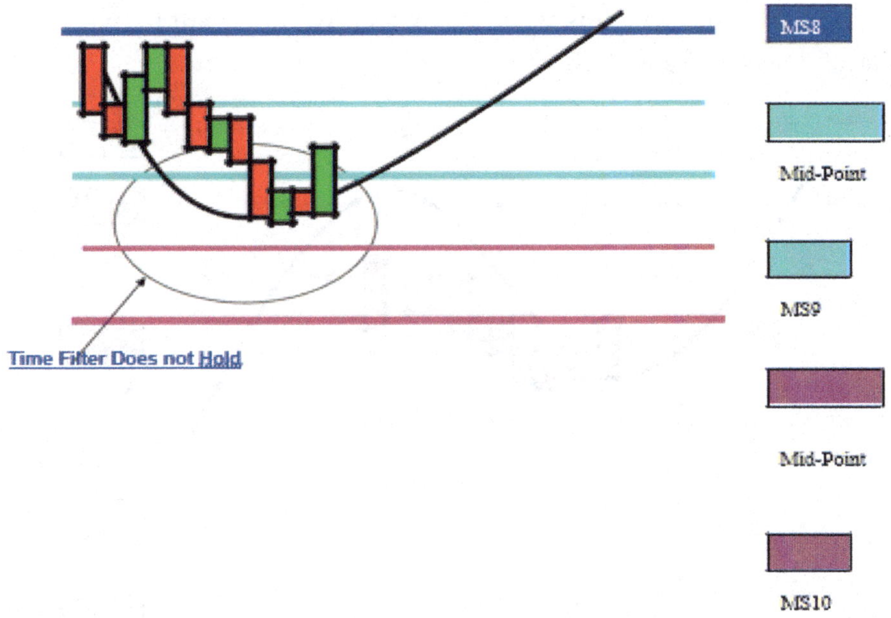

Rule # 35: **Bearish Trend Extension Zone; Distribution 3 (MS10 – MS11)**

If the candle body closes below the midpoint of MS4 & MS5, it indicates the market has extended the trend and will attempt to break below MS4 on the next wave down. Look to sell the 1st retracement after the close below the midpoint. Need to see 2 candles close higher then the high of the prior candle for true retracement. Then need to see a candle close lower then the low of the prior candle to generate the sell signal. The reason for this is this suggest the trend is shifting back to the downside, which is what we expect, we just want to make sure that it does before we sell.

Rule # 36: **Failed Bearish Trend Extension; Distribution 3 (MS10 – MS11)**

If the candle body fails to close below the midpoint of MS4 & MS5, and then a candle closes higher then the high of the prior candle this indicates a failed bearish trend extension and we look to buy limit 1 tick above the high of the prior candle or at the market for testing purposes. Then we expect the prices to revert towards the point of control or ZoneTrader Pivot.

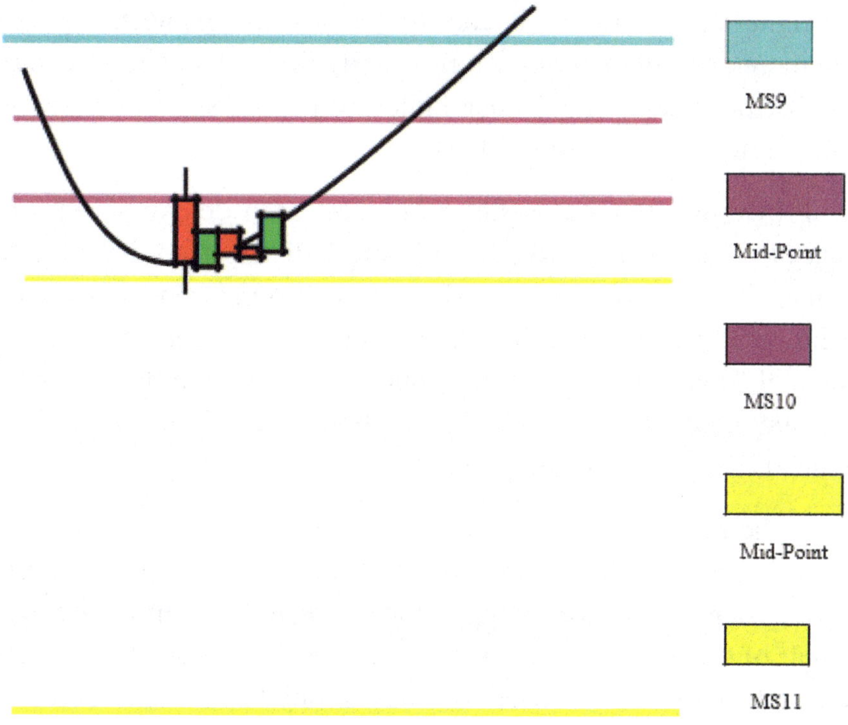

The persistence zone is the zone from the prior year, quarter, month, week, or day that the market spent the most time within. This can be calculated by counting the number of candles within each zone and determine the zone with the most candles residing within it. This zone meaning the prices of the top and the bottom of the zone become the persistence zone for the next year, quarter, month, week, and or day respectively and is represented by the two orange lines on any and all screenshots within this book.

Wherever the market spends the longest period of time is where the fight between the bulls and the bears is the greatest, suggesting and more even amount of the buyers and sellers. The persistence zone is what provides Zone-Trader Philosophy traders or followers with what i refer to as the control bias.

Providing the trader with the capability to determine who is in control of the market whether it's the bulls or bears on all 5 time frames. If the market opens inside the persistence zone then the there is no control bias and either the bulls or the bears must push prices above the top of the persistence zone or the bottom of the persistence and stay above the top or below the bottom and hold the time filter which is half of the opening range.

If the market opens inside the persistence zone then there is no control bias. In order for the bulls to take control of the market they must push prices above the top of the pz and hold the time filter which is half of the opening range if the bulls hold the time filter above the top of the pz then the trader will look to buy the first retracement. In order for the bears to take control of the market they must push prices below the bottom of the pz and hold the time filter and then the trader will look to sell the first retracement.

If the market opens above the top of the persistene zone then the bulls are in control of the market and trades favor the upside. In order for the bears to take back control of the market they will have to push prices completely through the PZ and hold the time filter below the bottom of the PZ and then the trader will then look to sell the first retracement.

If the market opens below the bottom of the persistence zone the bears are in control of the market and trades favor the downside. In order for the bulls to take control of the market they will have to push prices completely through the top of the PZ and hold the time filter above it and then the trader will look to buy the first retracement.

Whenever the control bias is in alignment with the directional bias the probability of winning increases. However, the more deviations the market moves above the top of the PZ and or below the bottom of the PZ.

The persistence zone deviations bands are plotted above and below the top and bottom of the PZ in orange dotted lines. The calculation for the persistence zone deviation bands are as follows:

TPZ1 = top of prior PZ

BPZ1 = bottom of prior PZ

TPZ2 = top of current PZ

BPZ2 = bottom of current PZ

TPZ1 - BPZ1 = A

TPZ2 - BPZ2 = B

A + B / 2 = C

Where C is the deviation value that is added to the top of the PZ 3 or more times dependent upon price movement and subtracted three or more times from the bottom of the PZ dependent upon price movement

Bullish Deviation 1 = TPZ2 + C

Bullish Deviation 2 = BD1 + C

Bullish Deviation 3 = BD2 + C

Bearish Deviation 1 (BED1) = BPZ2 - C

Bearish Deviation 2 (BED2) = BED1 - C

Bearish Deviation 3 (BED3) = BED2 – C

And so on and so forth.

The more deviations the market moves away from the top or bottom of the PZ the higher the probability that is reverts back towards them. So for example if the market is at the second deviation above the top of the persistence zone and then finds resistance from the third deviation, while simultaneously generating a bearish directional bias from generating a sell signal from rules 2, 4, 6...ect. Then the Zone-Trader can analyze this as being an alignment in directional and control bias, which thus forth increases the probability of winning and then they can expect bearish movement at least until either it reaches Bullish deviation 1 since this is now considered to be a support to market movement and or a bullish signal is generated by another Zone-trader rule.

This suggest that the trader will look for the price of the Bullish deviation 1 and look to see if it has alignment to any of the bearish zones within the distribution that It is residing, for example if the Bullish Deviation 1 resides around the midpoint of the Bearish Breakout zone on the weekly profile and the market has already failed to confirm an uptrend and found resistance at the Bullish Deviation 2 and has now reversed and is attempting to make a bearish breakout on the week, if the market finds support at the Bullish deviation 1 and fails to make a bearish breakout on the week then again the Zone-Trader can analyze this as once again having Control bias and Directional bias alignment.

Of course this employs common support/resistance analysis into the Zone-Trader methodology in the terms that if a resistance to the market is broken and thus becomes a support and will try to block the market from going lower and vice a versa a support to the market if broken thus becomes a resistance and will also attempt to block the market from going higher. Please keep in mind once again that support / resistance is a leading indicator especially if combined with patterns in price by using candlestick analysis like my trading methodology Zone-Trader Philosophy.

I have rarely seen the market exceed the third deviation above or below the top or bottom of the persistence zone, but the formula can be extended to a fourth or fifth deviation if need be. The higher the time frame profile the lower the probability of the market ever exceeding the third deviation. What this means is that the probability of the third deviation being broken in either the bullish or bearish direction on the Yearly Profile is lower than it would be on the Quarterly and so on and so forth sequentially.

The deviation bands can also be used to form clusters on the lower time frames in combination with any of the other support or resistances that are derived from my proprietary trading methodologies 3 distributions within all 5 profiles. The Zone-Trader can look at the prices that are within the average daily range of the top and bottom of the PZ and the deviation bands derived from them on the Yearly, Quarterly, Monthly, and Weekly profile and plot them on the daily profile using a specified color and look to see if they form a cluster, meaning the more support or resistance levels in one price area the lower the probability the market will break through it; however, if the market should break through it then I would look for strong trend to develop in that direction.

A Persistance Zone that was never broken meaning the market opened below it and never traded above the top of the PZ and held the time filter, or vice a versa the market opened above it and never traded below the bottom of the PZ and held the time filter then that persistence zone gets carried forward in time by tracing the prices using a horizontal line tool in Dark Green, Dark Maroon, or Dark Brown, and they will once again attempt to provide support or resistance to the market sometime in the future.

Dynamic methodology means that the methodology has the ability to adapt to all possible market conditions and the changes within them. All markets move from balanced state to a transitioning state, to a trending state, to a transitioning state, and back to a balanced state. These market mechanics that exist an auction based markets, cause other mechanical systems to break down over time, do to their ability to function well in one condition, but then as the market shifts into a new condition, the parameters for entry whether it be a buy or a sell order, create the failure because they are designed to take advantage of specific market movement and do not have the capability to to identify that the change in condition has occurred. They only search for specific parameters related to price, Volume. Open interest, overbought, oversold, volatility, strength of trend, but never all of these market internals all at the same time.

For example a system may work well in a trending market and then breakdown when the market goes into a reversal, or a sideways pattern, when fair prices are established. Most mechanical based systems lack the ability to determine a shift or change in the underlying condition of the market fast enough and therefore, lead to consecutive false signals to occur, which end up resulting in losing traders. The lower the time frame the system is being applied to the higher the percentage of false signals that will occur. A methodology that is dynamic has the capability to adapt to the market internals and utilized them to identify the current condition as well as the change from one condition to another, normally have some form of theory at the base, for example auction market theory, Dow theory, Elliott wave theory, and or market profile theory.

The application of my methodology that utilizes, auction market theory derived from support and resistance, on a multiple time frame perspective, is regarded as a fully dynamic trading methodology and provides me the trader with the capability to identify all current conditions upon five time frames, and all changes in direction that are occurring or expected to occur upon those time frames as well. This allows me the trader, the ability to adapt with them from position trader, to swing trader, and to day trader, or I can utilize them to just day trade period.

For example, of the Yearly profile has already established a bearish breakout, meaning a candle body close below the midpoint between MS1 and MS2, that footprint is now in the market and creates the ability for the market to go into a retracement phase much higher, which tells me to start looking for suggestions the retracement is under way from the lower time frames, and then retraced and is now attempting to confirm a downtrend. If the Quarterly Profile failed to make a bullish breakout, and has now already reverted back to the POC, and re-established a balanced state, them we will need to see the market trade below the ZT pivot and start attempting to breakout of a balanced oscillating state to the downside by establishing a candle body close before the midpoint between the ZT pivot and MS1, in order to fall in alignment with the Yearly profile of the Yearly had not already established the confirmation of the downtrend, however if the bearish trend confirmation is already established on the Yearly profile then we will need to see the ZT pivot provide support and push prices back in the bullish direction and attempt to break out of a balanced oscillating state to the upside, with a candle body close above the midpoint between the ZT pivot, and MR1.

Let's say hypothetically that the monthly, has failed to make a bullish breakout, reversed to the POC and then failed to make a bearish breakout, and now suggest that prices will start moving in the bullish direction as this suggest that mean reversion is under way and the market will revert back to the ZT pivot on the monthly profile and return to a balanced state, theoretically resuming fair prices. I would then look for bullish market movement to occur on my weekly profile, maybe the market is also failing to establish a bearish breakout, or confirm a downtrend, or maybe it is above the pivot and increasing in price, the point being any and all bullish market movement throughout that entire week, will provide me with the capability to take any and all buy signals on my daily profile, because at this point I now have alignment on a multi time frame basis.

Now the market begins to revert back to the point of control on the monthly profile, this movement may take at least one full wave to occur meaning prices move higher and then pull back slightly no more than .786 retracement of the first leg of the retracement phase, and then continue higher and head towards the POC. I would then expect the weekly profile to suggest that this formation of the second leg and or a full wave formation to occur on the monthly by finding resistance at the POC and then failing to breakout of a balanced oscillating state in the bearish direction, or maybe the market breakout of a balanced oscillating state on the weekly and then formulizes, a pivot bounce, or maybe the weekly makes a bullish breakout and then goes into a retracement phase.

All of these possible scenarios creates the outlook for me to look for bearish signals to occur on the daily profile, but to eventually to look for a failure to the downside in the philosophy to occur to signal that the race of the first leg move in the retracement phase of the monthly profile has ended, and now the next leg will revert back to the POC on the monthly, which at this point I can continue to take all the buy signals on the daily profile while acknowledging price areas that I might need to put on the brakes through the application of the ZT philosophy on the weekly profile.

Maybe the weekly already formed a pivot bounce and now is attempting to make a bullish breakout, then I would look for resistance around MR1 and again at the midpoint between MR1 and MR2, I would then need to correlate those to price levels in relationship to the ZT pivot on the monthly profile since the market is definitely going to touch that price most likely prior to the weekly being able to make a bullish breakout, but not necessarily. However this analysis will keep me in alignment with the changes in trend or in direction throughout the day session, for at least two days possibly even 3 or 4, as the weekly could get initial resistance at MR1 pull back slightly and then continue higher towards the midpoint of the bullish breakout zone's price level.

Then maybe the market fails to extend the bullish uptrend on the day which suggest it will revert back to the POC on the day, but then the day session closes, and tomorrow the market fails to make a bearish breakout and then reverts back to the ZT pivot, and then breaks out of balanced oscillation to the upside and then starts attempting to make a bullish breakout, I can theoretically take any and all of these buy signals, that are occurring in the daily profile. At this point the Quarterly Profile would have failed to breakout of a balanced oscillating state in the bearish direction and would now be attempting to breakout of one to the bullish direction, this would fall in line with the market going into a retracement phase on the Yearly profile, after establishing or confirming a bearish downtrend.

I would now look for failures to the upside on the Quarterly Profile, failed bullish breakout or a failed confirmation of an uptrend, this would suggest to me that the retracement phase on the Yearly was over and it was subsequently starting the next leg down in attempt to extend the bearish downtrend. Now that the market has returned to a balanced state on the monthly profile, it will now need to create a failure in the bullish direction, or establish the philosophy in the bearish direction. The failure may occur after the market breakouts of a balanced state in the bullish direction and then fails to make a bullish breakout, this would suggest that one wave to the upside and then start a leg to the downside or possibly formulize a wave formation to the downside as well.

This tells me to initially look for bullish movement on the weekly and then I could take any and all buy signals on the daily profile, until the weekly started to approach areas of resistance at prices that are in the same areas as the top of the balanced oscillation area on the monthly and on the Quarterly Profile, as well as the midpoint of the bullish breakout zone on both of those profiles prices as well. Look to identify where those prices fall within the weekly profile and see if there is alignment in the philosophy meaning maybe the prices at the midpoint of the bullish breakout zone of both the Quarterly and the monthly fall in alignment with MR1 on the weekly, or the top of the balanced oscillation area on the weekly, or possibly the midpoint of the bullish breakout zone as well, the point is wherever multiple resistance from multiple time frames is occurring at is most likely where we will eventually see the market find resistance and go into either a retracement phase, or a mean reversion phase on the Quarterly Profile and on the monthly profile.

Signaling that the retracement phase on the Yearly profile is over if it already established a confirmation of a downtrend, if the Yearly failed to confirm a downtrend, them I would expect the Quarterly and or monthly to establish bullish breakout, since the failure on the Yearly profile suggest the market will revert back to the ZT pivot on this time frame which may represent a move of 40 to 80 points possibly.

Let's say hypothetically that the Yearly failed to confirm a downtrend and is now reverting back to the ZT pivot, this move will most likely take at least one full wave formation, out possibly two. This means at least 4 to 8 legs of price movement being plotted via the application of a weekly candle, meaning each candlestick represents one full week of trading. Within each of these legs, the market will plot at least one wave formation on the Quarterly Profile, and most likely 2 or 3 formations on the monthly, which would lead to at least 4 formations on the weekly profile.

This means price will change direction at least 4 times prior to the Yearly profile reaching the ZT pivot, or reverting back to the mean or POC. Knowing this ahead of time helps to allow us to take advantage of these price swings, since we know that traders favor the long-term direction of the market, however as a day trader I will still be too make money via counter trend signals, as long as I have alignment between the monthly and the weekly profiles. But keep in mind that the breakout and trend confirmation signals are going to be a higher probability of winning then the trend extension trades. Look to see where the daily profile has alignment with the .618 or the .786

retracement price, this will help to predict the expected philosophy that might occur on the weekly profile, and whether the confirmation of a downtrend signal or the trend extension signal will fail in the bearish direction on the daily. But keep in mind if I wait for the failure to occur on the daily to the downside then the buy signal will result in the highest probability of winning, since it creates a re-alignment in direction between the monthly and the Yearly profile in regard to the overall trend and expected price movement, also it will or may result in a larger profit since the predicted future price movement, places initial target at the POC of the daily profile, then at the ZT pivot of the monthly profile would be the second target.

Once the market reaches the ZT pivot of the monthly profile, Theni must look for resistance to occur and put the brakes on buy signals, unless the market breaks above the POC and continues higher attempting to breakout of a balanced oscillation state, and the weekly profile is also suggesting higher prices to occur then I can continue to take buy signals on the daily profile, since I expect the market to eventually reach the POC on the Yearly profile or that profiles ZT pivot.

APPENDIX A

On the Yearly Profile which again is analyzed using a Weekly candle the market was able to break above MR4 and into the 2nd Distribution (MR4 to MR11), and trades up into the Bearish Confirmation Zone of this distribution, which denoted from MR5 to MR6. The market then forms a top after we see a close lower than the low of the prior candle. The trader can see that at this point based upon Zone-Trader Philosophy that the market has now confirmed a downtrend in distribution 2 and will next make an attempt to extend the bearish downtrend by forming a candle body close below the midpoint between (MR5 to MR4). If the market cannot establish a candle body close below the midpoint of the bearish trend extension zone of distribution 2, then the uptrend will continue higher attempting to reach the zone-trader pivot of distribution 2 or the midpoint of the Neutral zone MR7 to MR8. However, the market is able to establish the bearish trend extension of distribution signaling a reversal in the Gold Market is Underway! At this point the Zone-Trader would look to sell the first retracement which generated a signal at 1770.48. At this point the zone-trader must expect the market to trade lower back into distribution 1 and retest the now support being generated by MR2 the bottom of the Bullish Confirmation Zone of distribution 1, where the market was able to establish an uptrend within the current Year or current profile. At this point the zone-trader would expect the market to find support, and then make an attempt to re-extend the bullish uptrend of distribution 1 by establishing a candle body close above the midpoint between MR3 and MR4, if the market cannot extend the bullish uptrend of distribution 1 the zone-trader would then expect the market to continue and reach the point of control or the zone-trader pivot of distribution 1. Again based upon this chart that signaled a reversal in the Gold market in the third week of September 2011, the sell signal generated at 1770.48 and MR2 price was at 1377.45 a move of 393 points or $39,300 per contract; however i this move continued lower and eventually went into a bear market.*

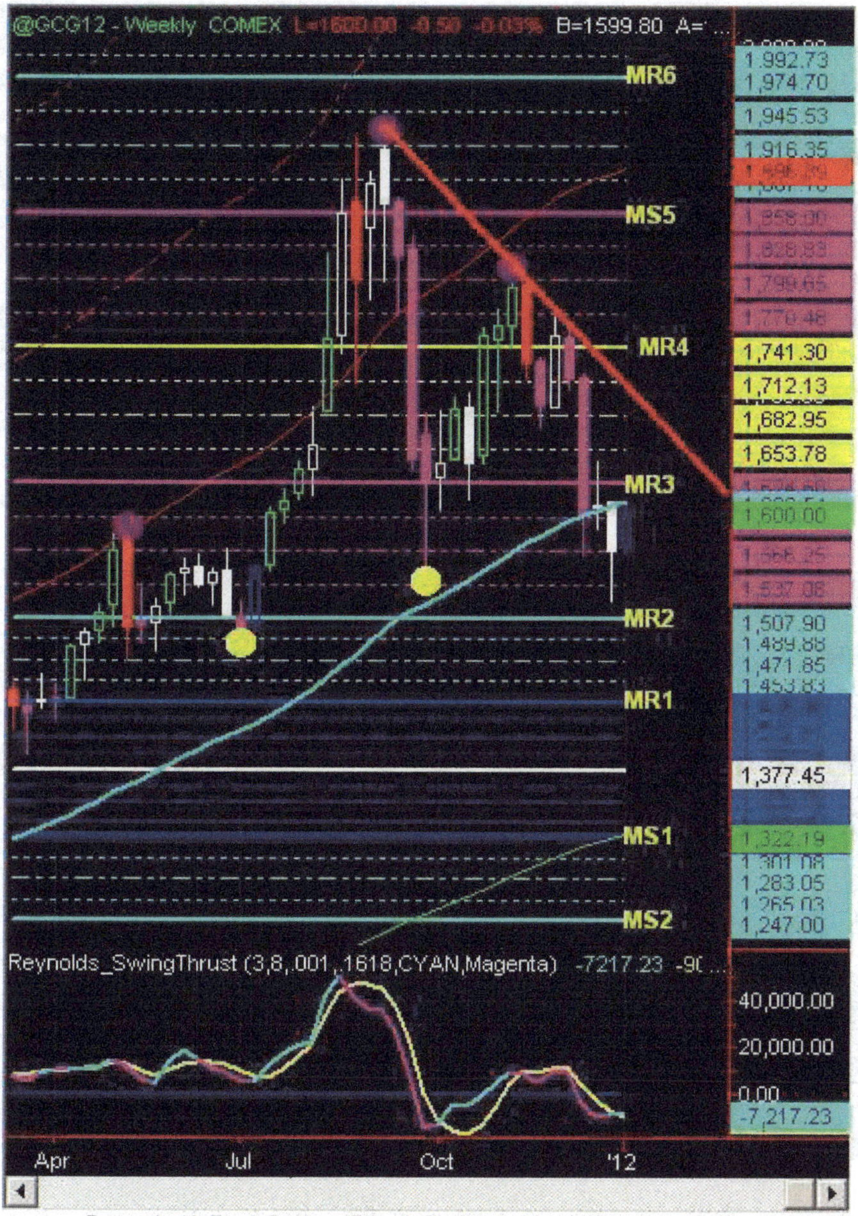

@GCG12 - Weekly COMEX
B=1599.80 A=
MR6
MS5
MR4
MR3
MR2
MR1
MS1
MS2
1,992.73
1,974.70
1,945.53
1,916.35
1,741.30
1,712.13
1,682.95
1,653.78
1,600.00
1,507.90
1,489.88
1,471.85
1,377.45
1,322.19
1,283.05
1,247.00
Reynolds_SwingThrust (3,8,.001,.1618,CYAN,Magenta) -7217.23
40,000.00
20,000.00
0.00
-7,217.23
Apr
Jul
Oct
'12

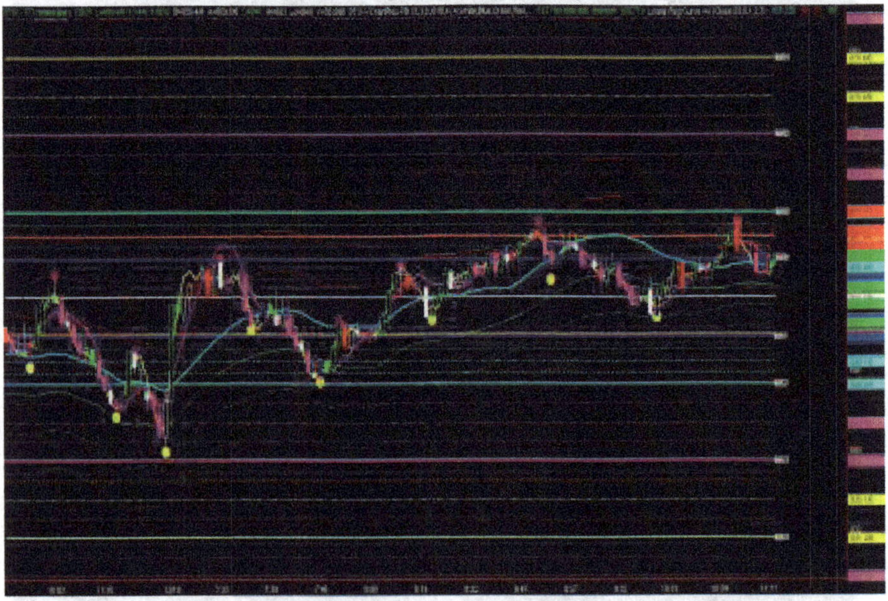

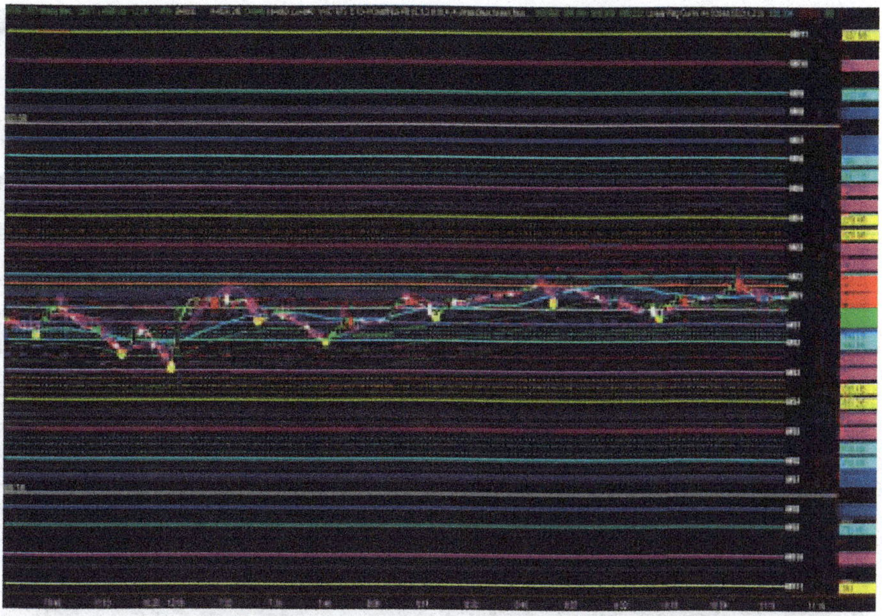

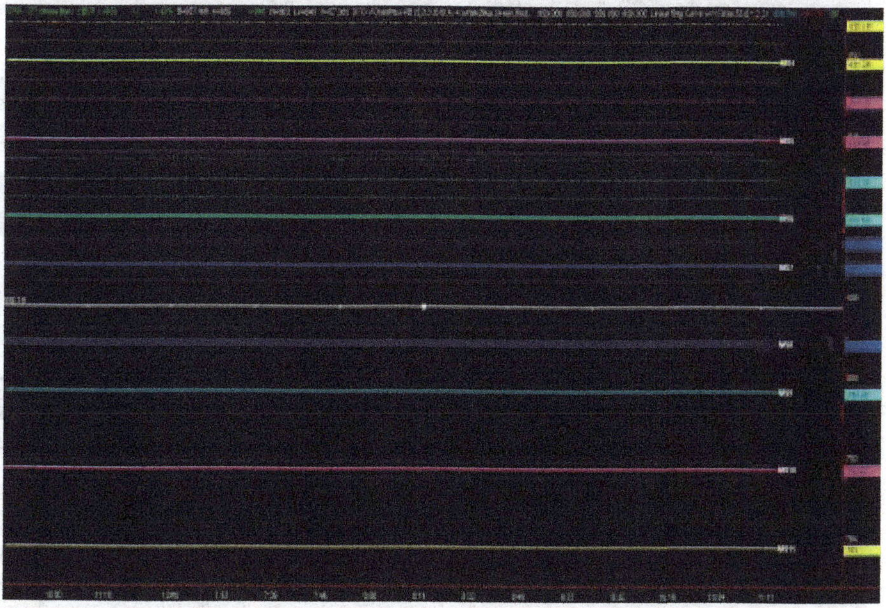

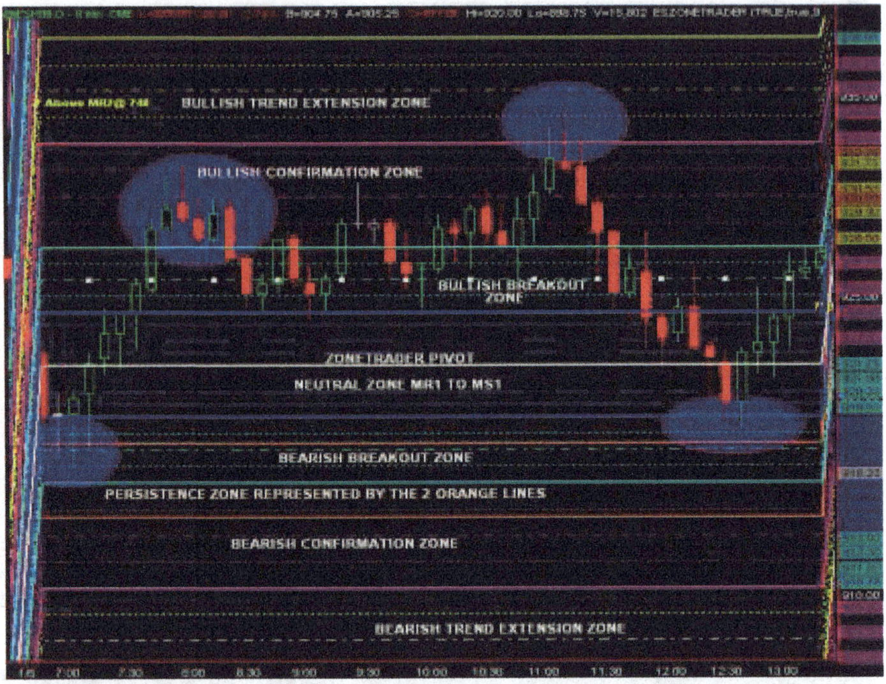
BULLISH TREND EXTENSION ZONE
BULLISH CONFIRMATION ZONE
BULLISH BREAKOUT ZONE
ZONETRADER PIVOT
NEUTRAL ZONE MR1 TO MS1
BEARISH BREAKOUT ZONE
PERSISTENCE ZONE REPRESENTED BY THE 2 ORANGE LINES
BEARISH CONFIRMATION ZONE
BEARISH TREND EXTENSION ZONE

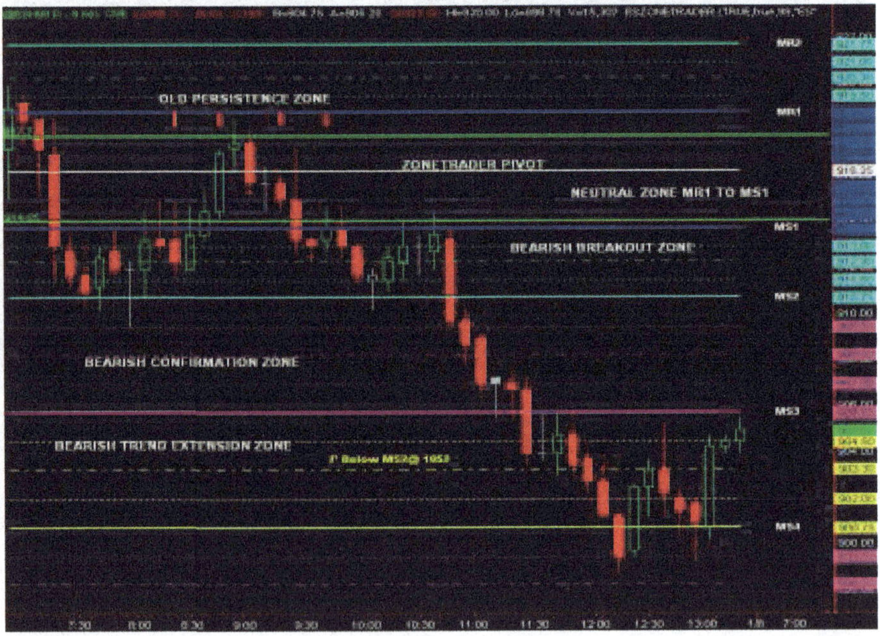
MR2
OLD PERSISTENCE ZONE
MR1
ZONETRADER PIVOT
NEUTRAL ZONE MR1 TO MS1
MS1
BEARISH BREAKOUT ZONE
MS2
BEARISH CONFIRMATION ZONE
MS3
BEARISH TREND EXTENSION ZONE
MS4

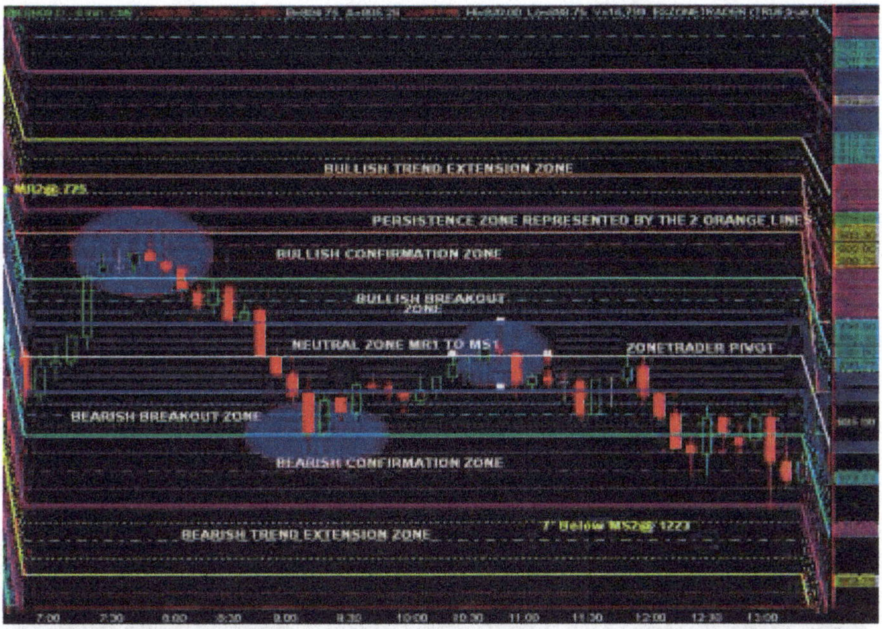

BULLISH TREND EXTENSION ZONE
PERSISTENCE ZONE REPRESENTED BY THE 2 ORANGE LINES
BULLISH CONFIRMATION ZONE
BULLISH BREAKOUT ZONE
NEUTRAL ZONE MR1 TO MS1
ZONETRADER PIVOT
BEARISH BREAKOUT ZONE
BEARISH CONFIRMATION ZONE
BEARISH TREND EXTENSION ZONE

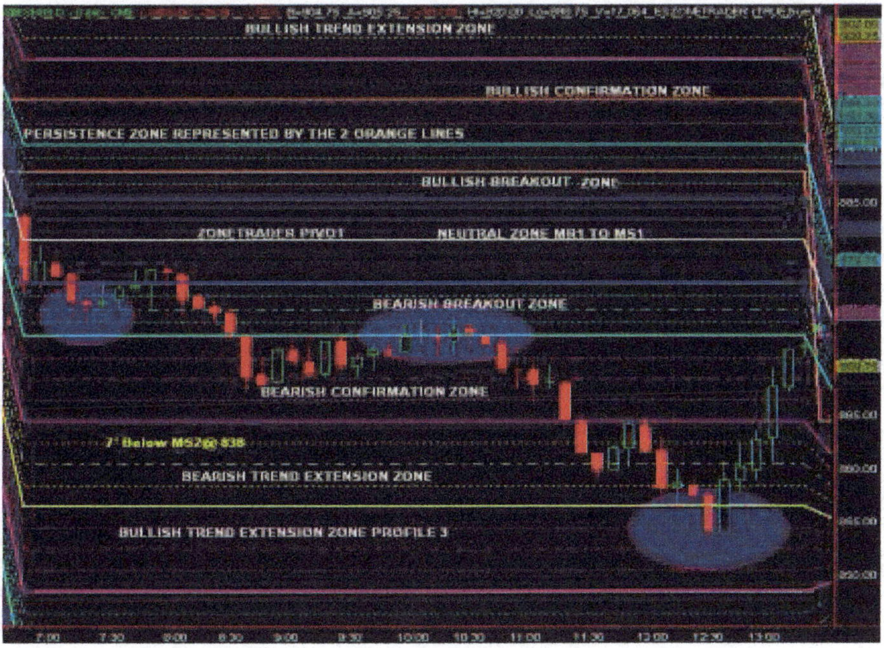

BULLISH TREND EXTENSION ZONE
BULLISH CONFIRMATION ZONE
PERSISTENCE ZONE REPRESENTED BY THE 2 ORANGE LINES
BULLISH BREAKOUT ZONE
ZONETRADER PIVOT
NEUTRAL ZONE MR1 TO MS1
BEARISH BREAKOUT ZONE
BEARISH CONFIRMATION ZONE
BEARISH TREND EXTENSION ZONE
BULLISH TREND EXTENSION ZONE PROFILE 3

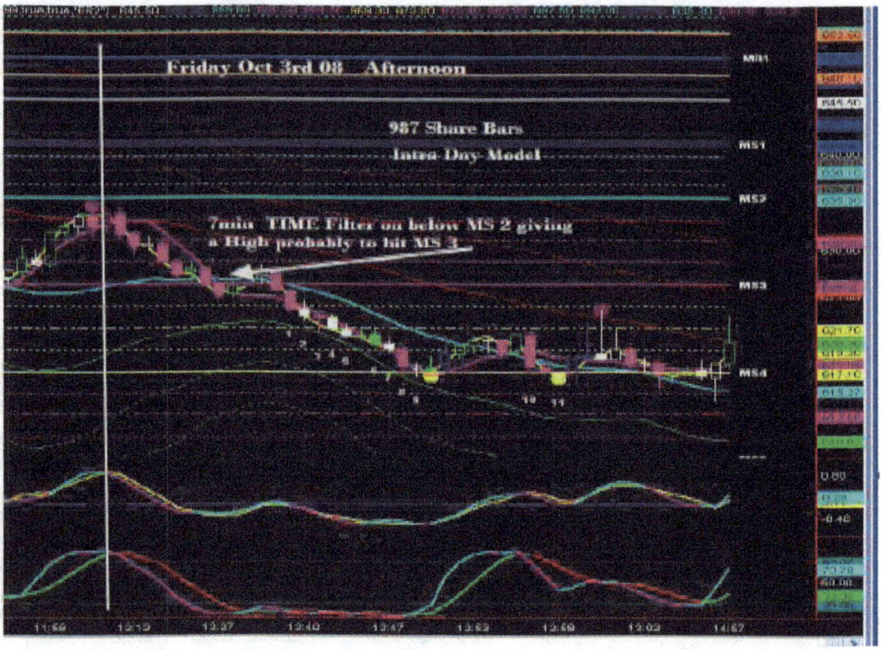
Friday Oct 3rd 08 Afternoon
987 Share Bars
Intra Day Model
7min TIME Filter on below MS 2 giving
a High probably to hit MS 3

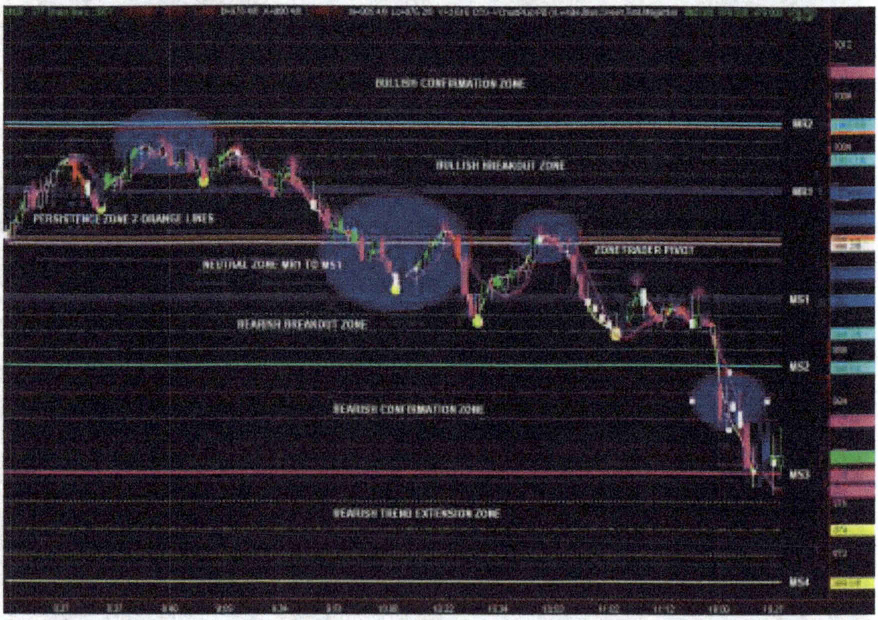
BULLISH CONFIRMATION ZONE
BULLISH BREAKOUT ZONE
PERSISTENCE ZONE 2 ORANGE LINES
NEUTRAL ZONE MR1 TO MS1
ZONE TRADER PIVOT
BEARISH BREAKOUT ZONE
BEARISH CONFIRMATION ZONE
BEARISH TREND EXTENSION ZONE

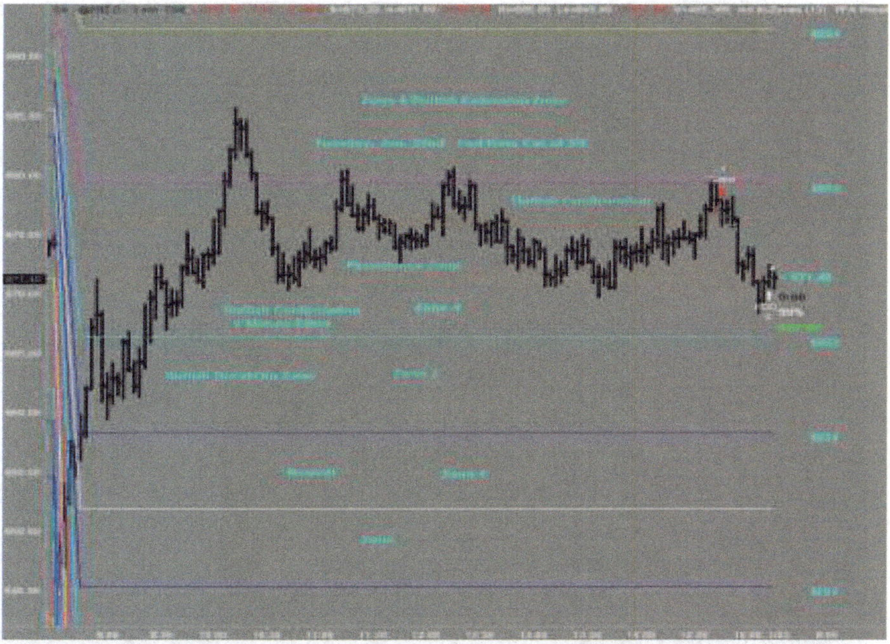

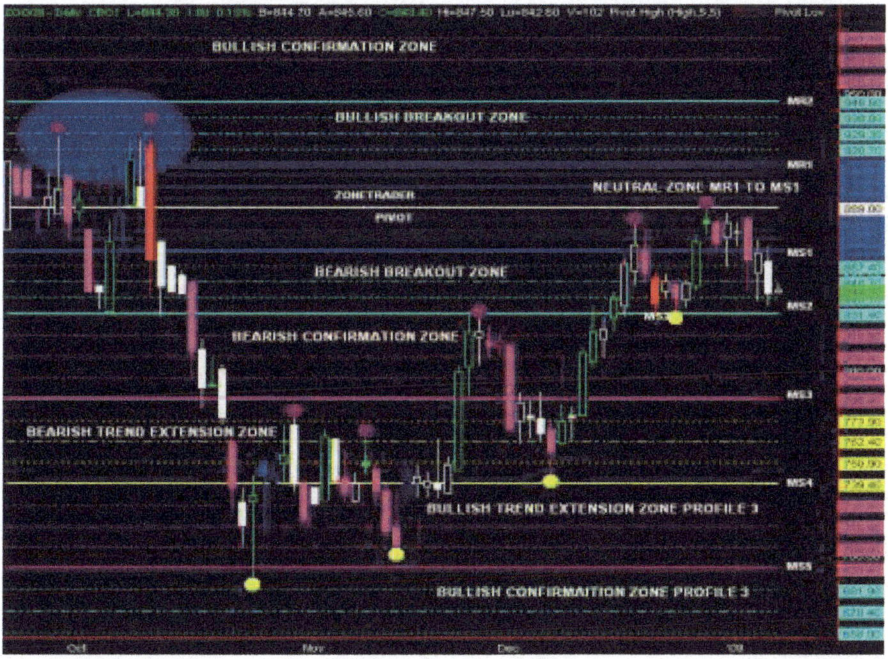
BULLISH CONFIRMATION ZONE
BULLISH BREAKOUT ZONE
MR2
MR1
ZONETRADER
PIVOT
NEUTRAL ZONE MR1 TO MS1
MS1
BEARISH BREAKOUT ZONE
MS2
BEARISH CONFIRMATION ZONE
MS3
BEARISH TREND EXTENSION ZONE
MS4
BULLISH TREND EXTENSION ZONE PROFILE 3
MS5
BULLISH CONFIRMAITION ZONE PROFILE 3
Oct
Nov
Dec

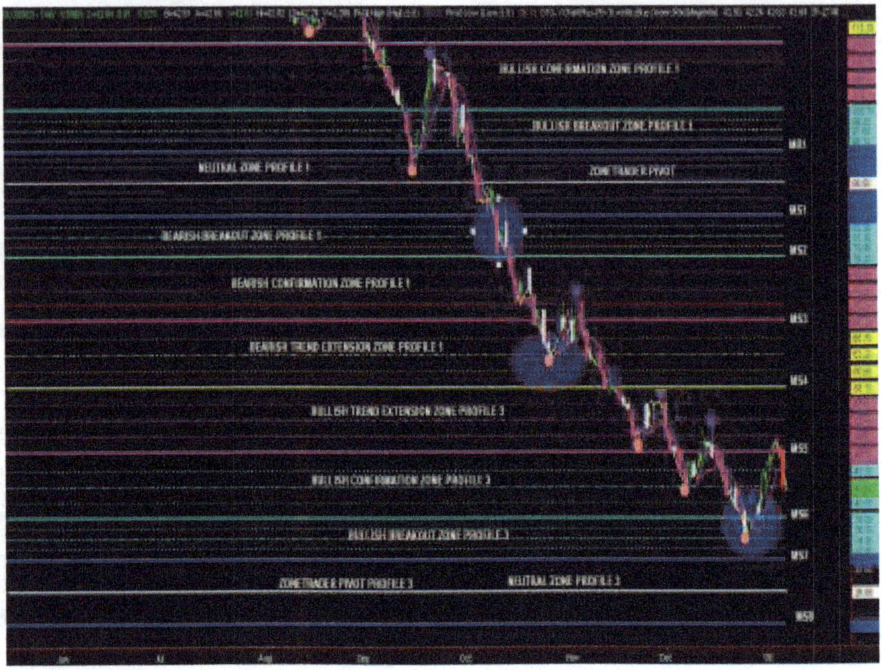
BULLISH CONFIRMATION ZONE PROFILE 1
BULLISH BREAKOUT ZONE PROFILE 1
NEUTRAL ZONE PROFILE 1
ZONETRADER PIVOT
BEARISH BREAKOUT ZONE PROFILE 1
BEARISH CONFIRMATION ZONE PROFILE 1
BEARISH TREND EXTENSION ZONE PROFILE 1
BULLISH TREND EXTENSION ZONE PROFILE 3
BULLISH CONFIRMATION ZONE PROFILE 3
BULLISH BREAKOUT ZONE PROFILE 3
ZONETRADER PIVOT PROFILE 3
NEUTRAL ZONE PROFILE 3

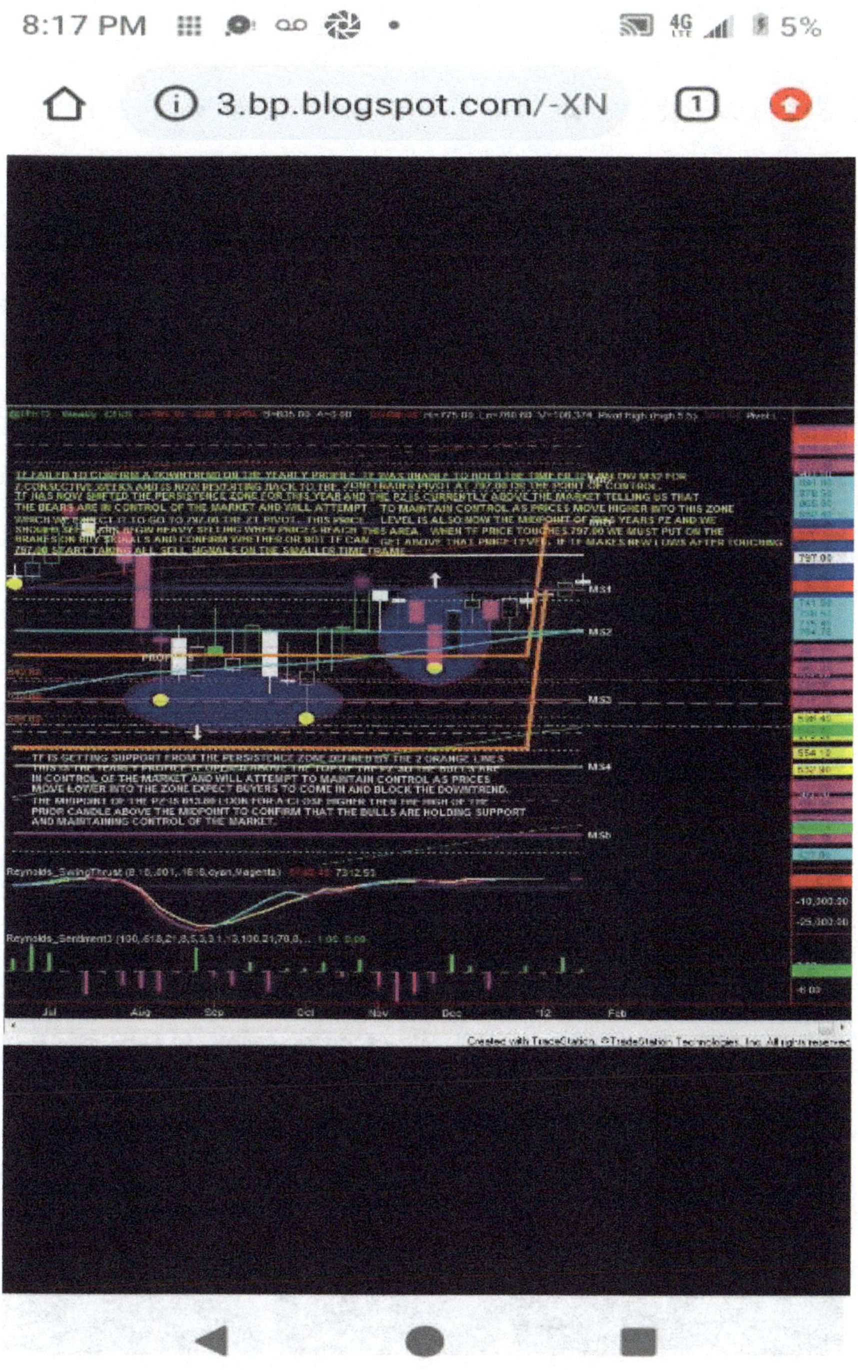
8:17 PM
5%
3.bp.blogspot.com/-XN
TF HAS NOW SHIFTED THE PERSISTENCE ZONE FOR THIS YEAR AND THE PZ IS CURRENTLY ABOVE THE MARKET TELLING US THAT
THE BEARS ARE IN CONTROL OF THE MARKET AND WILL ATTEMPT TO MAINTAIN CONTROL AS PRICES MOVE HIGHER INTO THIS ZONE
WHEN TF PRICE TOUCHES 797.00 WE MUST PUT ON THE
M31
M32
M33
M34
M35
IN CONTROL OF THE MARKET AND WILL ATTEMPT TO MAINTAIN CONTROL AS PRICES
MOVE LOWER INTO THE ZONE EXPECT BUYERS TO COME IN AND BLOCK THE DOWNTREND.
PRIOR CANDLE ABOVE THE MIDPOINT TO CONFIRM THAT THE BULLS ARE HOLDING SUPPORT
AND MAINTAINING CONTROL OF THE MARKET.
797.00
Jul
Aug
Sep
Oct
Nov
Dec
12
Feb
Created with TradeStation. ©TradeStation Technologies, Inc. All rights reserved.

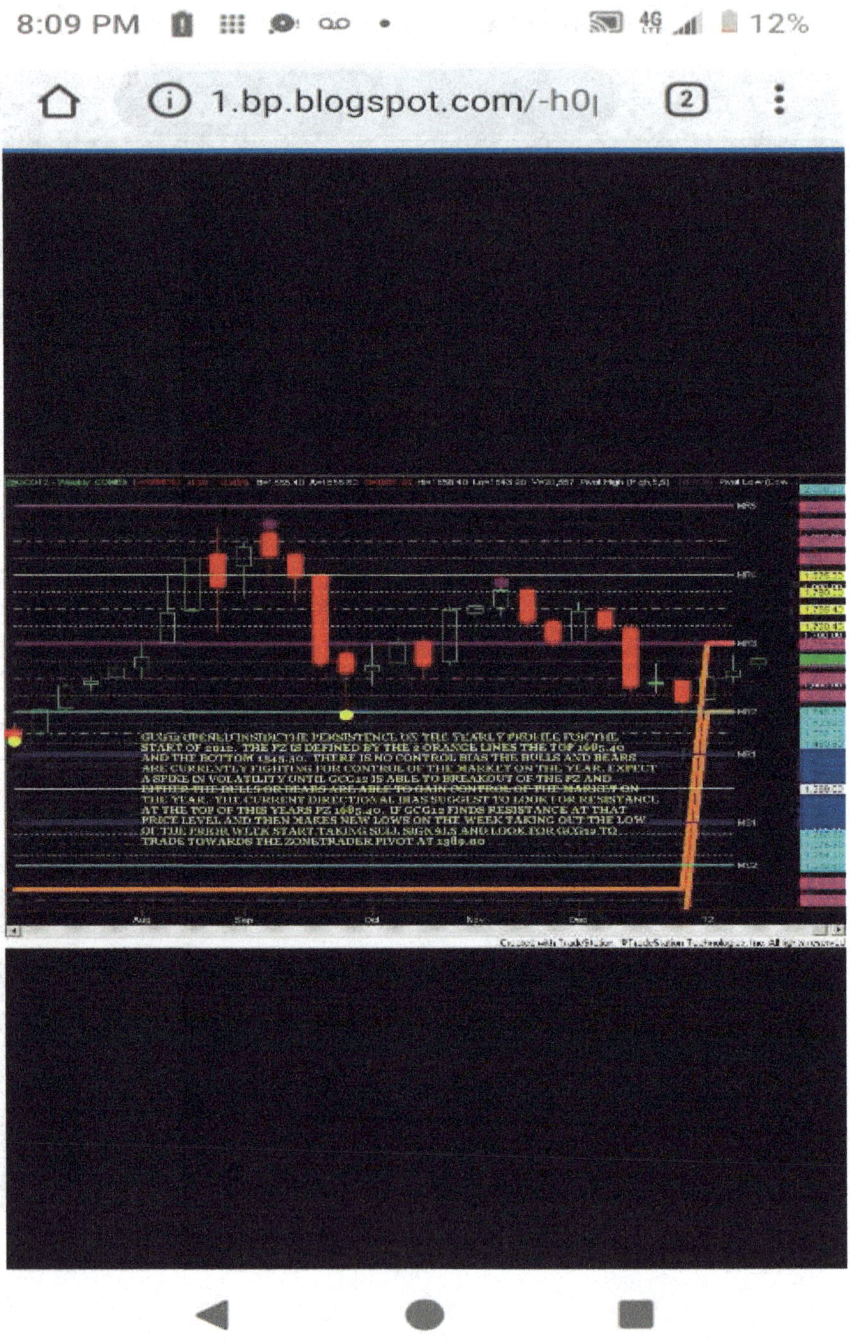
8:09 PM
12%
1.bp.blogspot.com/-h0
START OF 2012. THE FZ IS DEFINED BY THE 2 ORANGE LINES THE TOP 1605.40
AND THE BOTTOM 1545.40. THERE IS NO CONTROL BIAS THE BULLS AND BEARS
A SPIKE IN VOLATILITY UNTIL GCG12 IS ABLE TO BREAKOUT OF THE FZ AND
AT THE TOP OF THIS YEARS FZ 1605.40. IF GCG12 FINDS RESISTANCE AT THAT
PRICE LEVEL AND THEN MAKES NEW LOWS ON THE WEEK TAKING OUT THE LOW
TRADE TOWARDS THE ZONETRADER PIVOT AT 1589.40
Aug
Sep
Oct
Nov
Dec

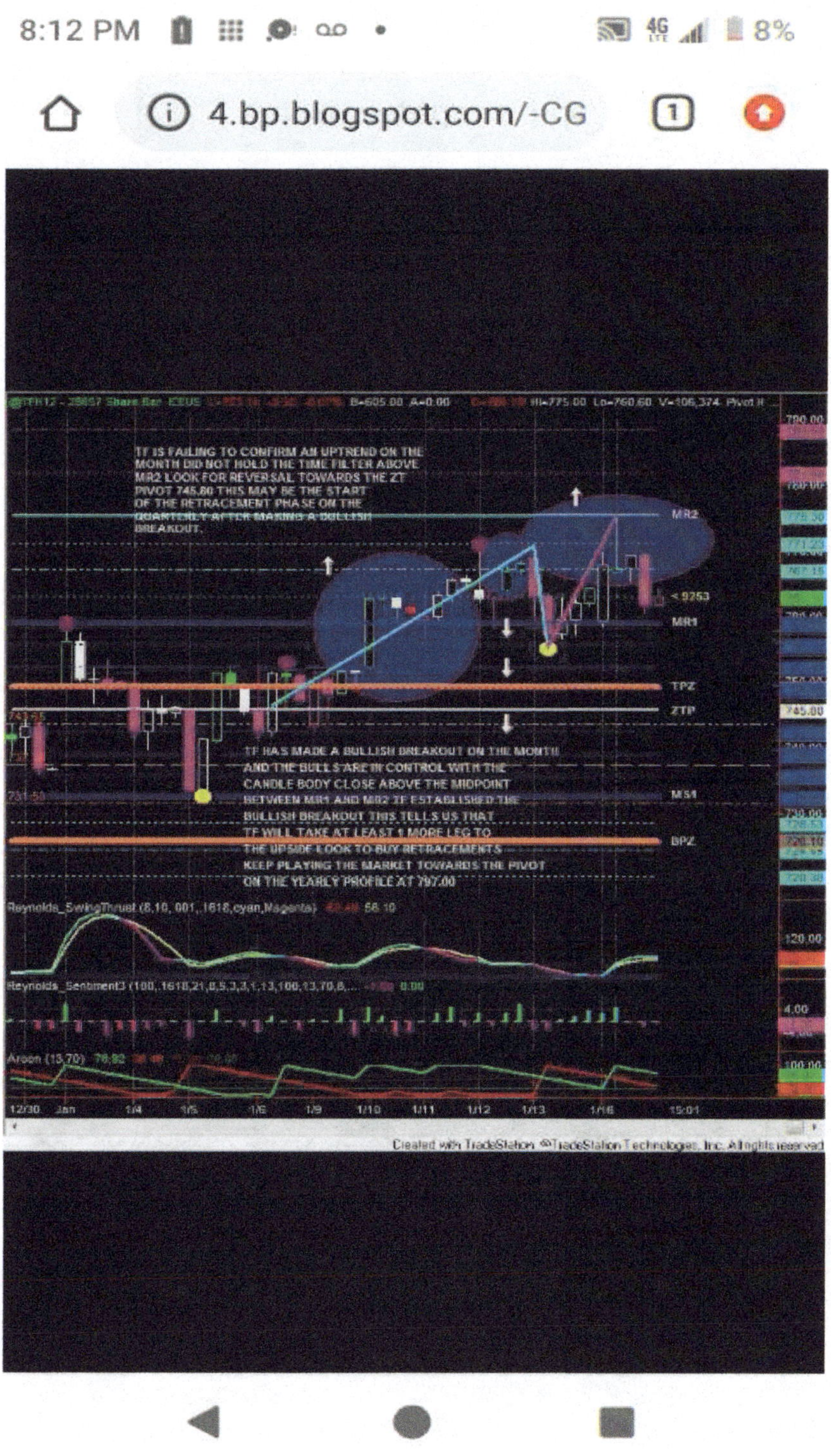
8:12 PM
8%
4.bp.blogspot.com/-CG
TF IS FAILING TO CONFIRM AN UPTREND ON THE MONTH DID NOT HOLD THE TIME FILTER ABOVE MR2 LOOK FOR REVERSAL TOWARDS THE ZT PIVOT 745.80 THIS MAY BE THE START OF THE RETRACEMENT PHASE ON THE QUARTERLY AFTER MAKING A BULLISH BREAKOUT.
MR2
MR1
TPZ
ZTP
MS1
BPZ
TF HAS MADE A BULLISH BREAKOUT ON THE MONTH AND THE BULLS ARE IN CONTROL WITH THE CANDLE BODY CLOSE ABOVE THE MIDPOINT BETWEEN MR1 AND MR2 TF ESTABLISHED THE BULLISH BREAKOUT THIS TELLS US THAT TF WILL TAKE AT LEAST 1 MORE LEG TO THE UPSIDE LOOK TO BUY RETRACEMENTS KEEP PLAYING THE MARKET TOWARDS THE PIVOT ON THE YEARLY PROFILE AT 797.00
B=605.00 A=0.00
Hi=775.00 Lo=760.60 V=106,374
Reynolds_SwingThrust
Reynolds_Sentiment3
Aroon (13,70)
Created with TradeStation ©TradeStation Technologies, Inc. All rights reserved

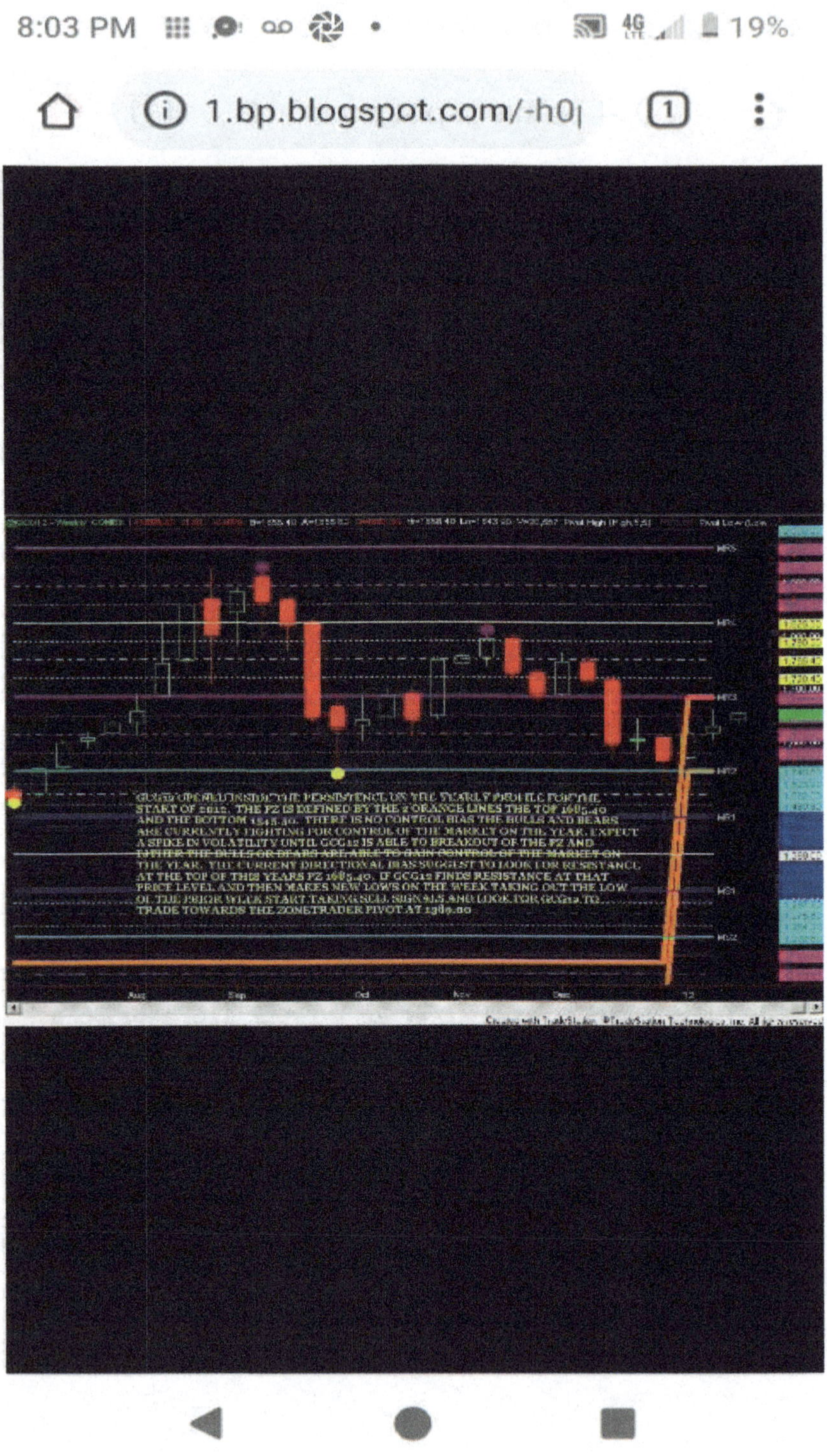
8:03 PM
19%
1.bp.blogspot.com/-h0
START OF 2012. THE PZ IS DEFINED BY THE 2 ORANGE LINES THE TOP 1685.40
AND THE BOTTOM 1545.40. THERE IS NO CONTROL BIAS THE BULLS AND BEARS
ARE CURRENTLY FIGHTING FOR CONTROL OF THE MARKET ON THE YEAR. EXPECT
A SPIKE IN VOLATILITY UNTIL GCG12 IS ABLE TO BREAKOUT OF THE PZ AND
AT THE TOP OF THIS YEARS PZ 1685.40. IF GCG12 FINDS RESISTANCE AT THAT
PRICE LEVEL AND THEN MAKES NEW LOWS ON THE WEEK TAKING OUT THE LOW
TRADE TOWARDS THE ZONETRADER PIVOT AT 1380.00

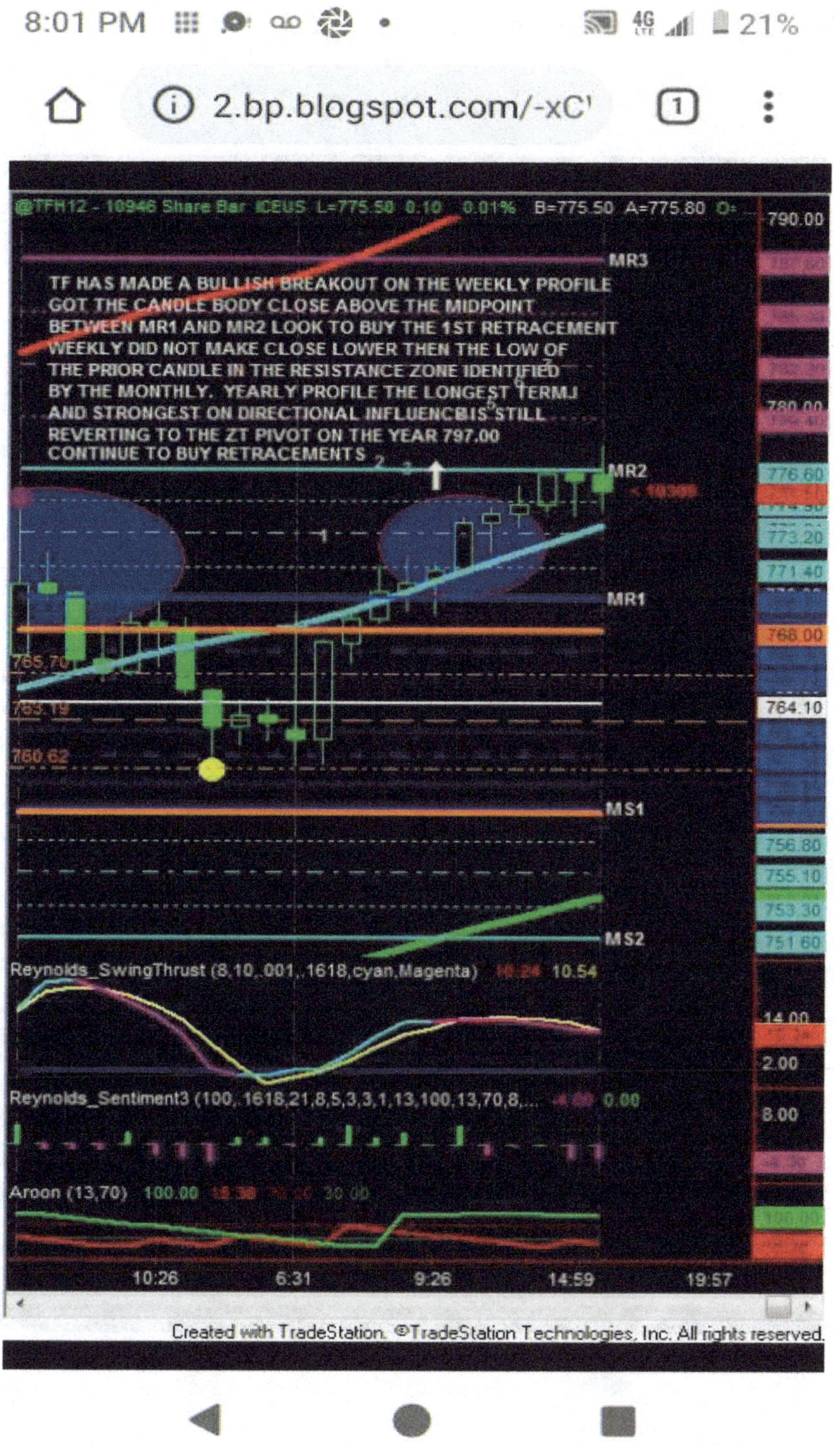
8:01 PM
21%
2.bp.blogspot.com/-xC
B=775.50 A=775.80
790.00
MR3
TF HAS MADE A BULLISH BREAKOUT ON THE WEEKLY PROFILE
GOT THE CANDLE BODY CLOSE ABOVE THE MIDPOINT
BETWEEN MR1 AND MR2 LOOK TO BUY THE 1ST RETRACEMENT
WEEKLY DID NOT MAKE CLOSE LOWER THEN THE LOW OF
THE PRIOR CANDLE IN THE RESISTANCE ZONE IDENTIFIED
BY THE MONTHLY. YEARLY PROFILE THE LONGEST TERMJ
AND STRONGEST ON DIRECTIONAL INFLUENCBIS STILL
REVERTING TO THE ZT PIVOT ON THE YEAR 797.00
CONTINUE TO BUY RETRACEMENTS
MR2
776.60
773.20
771.40
MR1
768.00
765.70
764.10
763.19
760.62
MS1
756.80
755.10
753.30
MS2
751.60
Reynolds_SwingThrust (8,10,.001,.1618,cyan,Magenta) 10.54
14.00
2.00
Reynolds_Sentiment3 (100,.1618,21,8,5,3,3,1,13,100,13,70,8,...
8.00
Aroon (13,70) 100.00
10:26
6:31
9:26
14:59
19:57
Created with TradeStation. ©TradeStation Technologies, Inc. All rights reserved.

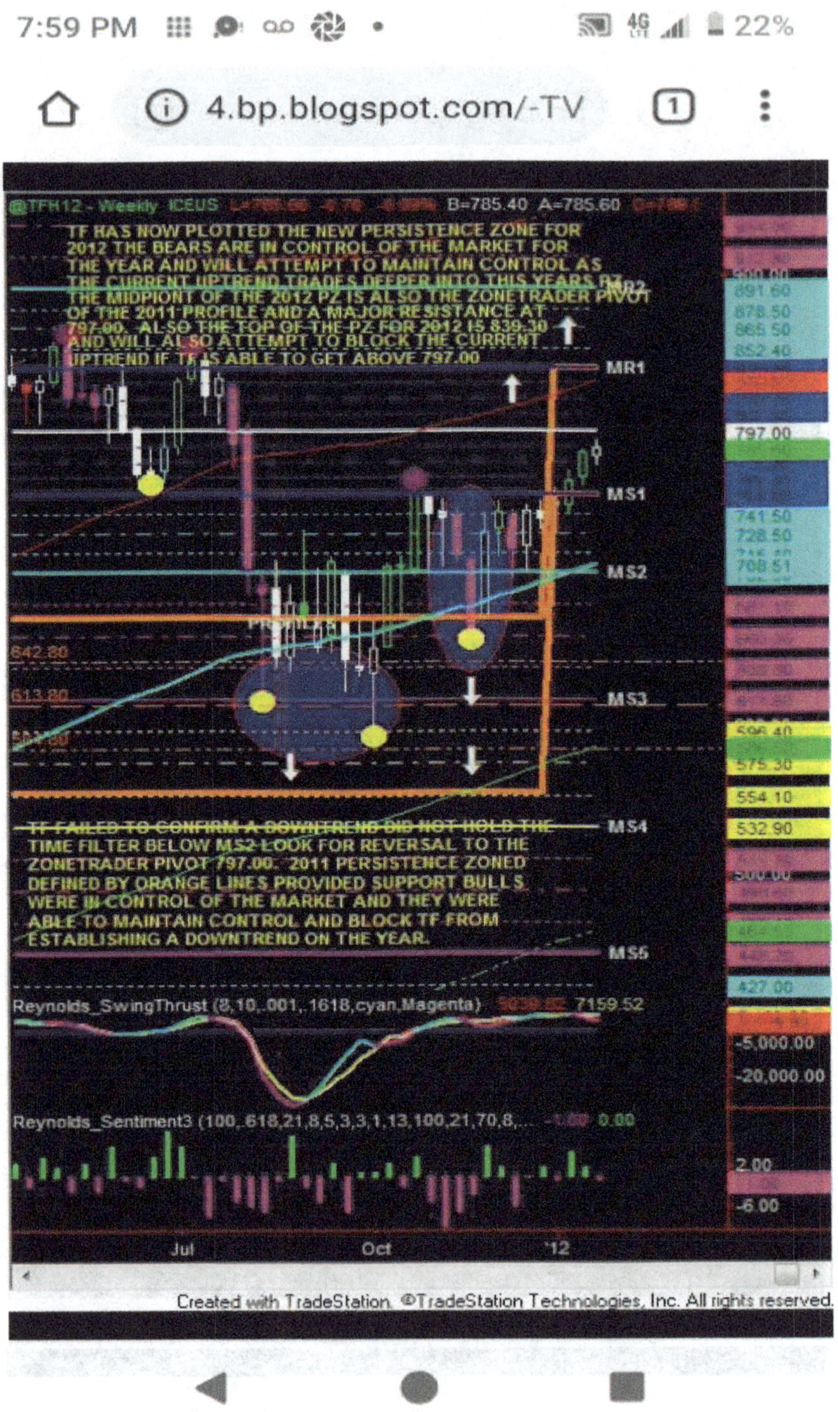
7:59 PM
22%
4.bp.blogspot.com/-TV
@TFH12 - Weekly ICEUS
B=785.40 A=785.60
TF HAS NOW PLOTTED THE NEW PERSISTENCE ZONE FOR 2012 THE BEARS ARE IN CONTROL OF THE MARKET FOR THE YEAR AND WILL ATTEMPT TO MAINTAIN CONTROL AS THE CURRENT UPTREND TRADES DEEPER INTO THIS YEARS PZ THE MIDPIONT OF THE 2012 PZ IS ALSO THE ZONETRADER PIVOT OF THE 2011 PROFILE AND A MAJOR RESISTANCE AT 797.00. ALSO THE TOP OF THE PZ FOR 2012 IS 839.30 AND WILL ALSO ATTEMPT TO BLOCK THE CURRENT UPTREND IF TF IS ABLE TO GET ABOVE 797.00
MR2
MR1
MS1
MS2
MS3
MS4
MS5
891.60
878.50
865.50
852.40
797.00
741.50
728.50
708.51
642.80
613.80
596.40
575.30
554.10
532.90
427.00
TF FAILED TO CONFIRM A DOWNTREND DID NOT HOLD THE TIME FILTER BELOW MS2 LOOK FOR REVERSAL TO THE ZONETRADER PIVOT 797.00. 2011 PERSISTENCE ZONED DEFINED BY ORANGE LINES PROVIDED SUPPORT BULLS WERE IN CONTROL OF THE MARKET AND THEY WERE ABLE TO MAINTAIN CONTROL AND BLOCK TF FROM ESTABLISHING A DOWNTREND ON THE YEAR.
Reynolds_SwingThrust (8,10,.001,.1618,cyan,Magenta) 7159.52
-5,000.00
-20,000.00
Reynolds_Sentiment3 (100,.618,21,8,5,3,3,1,13,100,21,70,8,... 0.00
2.00
-6.00
Jul
Oct
'12
Created with TradeStation. ©TradeStation Technologies, Inc. All rights reserved.

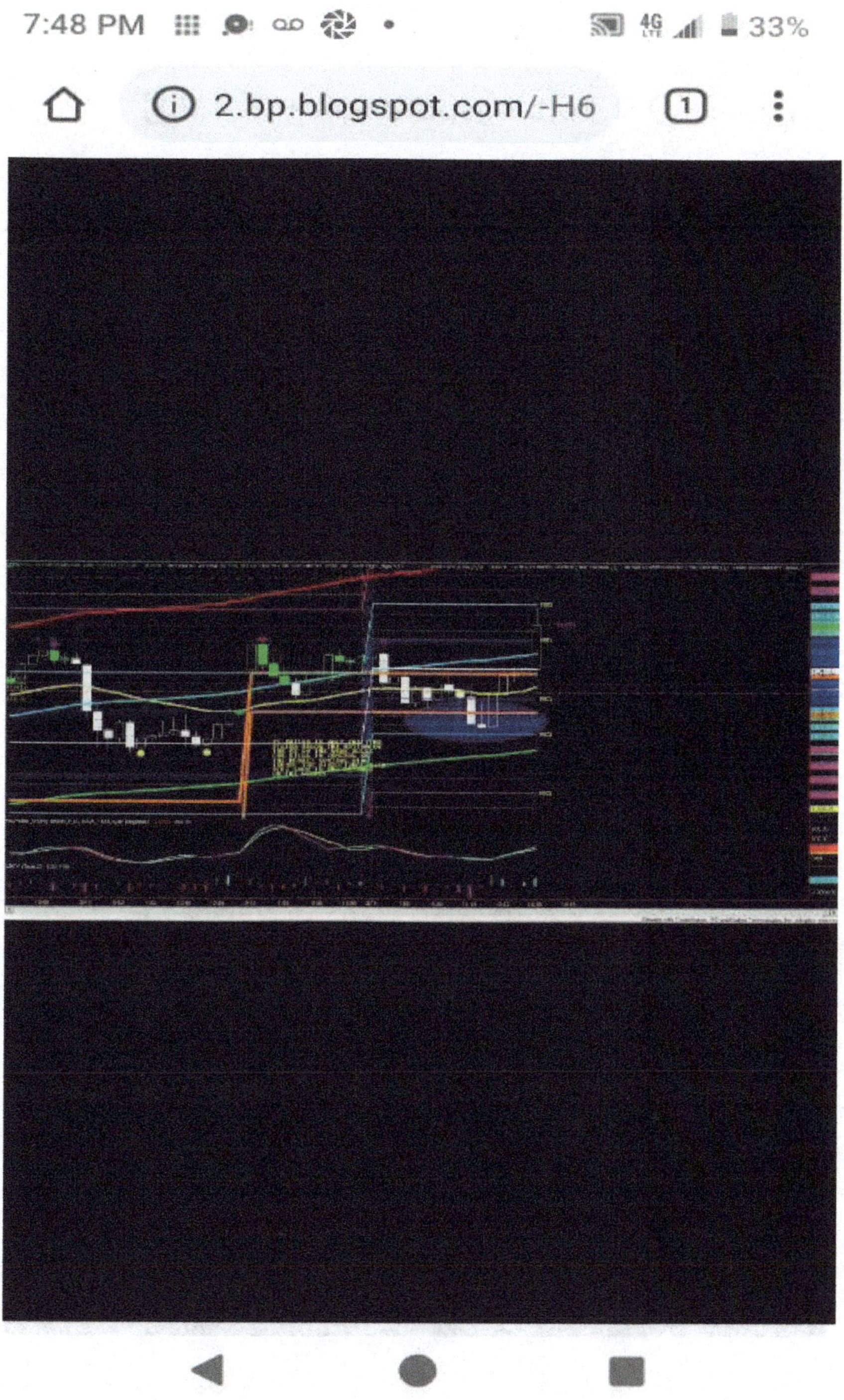
7:48 PM
4G
33%
2.bp.blogspot.com/-H6
1

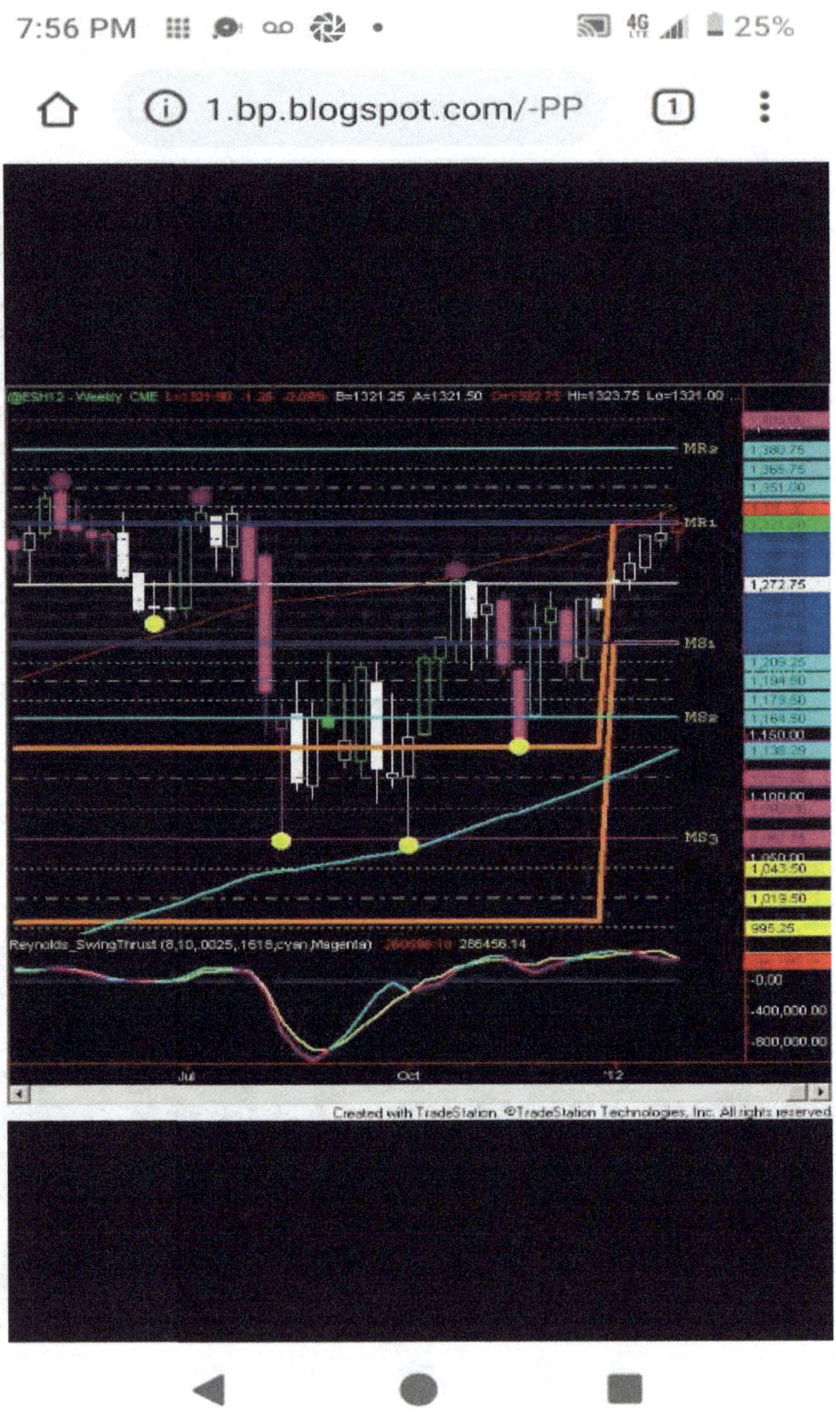
7:56 PM
25%
1.bp.blogspot.com/-PP
@ESH12 - Weekly CME
B=1321.25 A=1321.50
HI=1323.75 Lo=1321.00
MR2
MR1
MS1
MS2
MS3
1,380.75
1,365.75
1,351.00
1,272.75
1,209.25
1,194.50
1,179.50
1,164.50
1,150.00
1,100.00
1,043.50
1,019.50
995.25
Reynolds_SwingThrust (8,10,.0025,.1618,cyan,Magenta)
286456.14
0.00
-400,000.00
-800,000.00
Jul
Oct
'12
Created with TradeStation ©TradeStation Technologies, Inc. All rights reserved

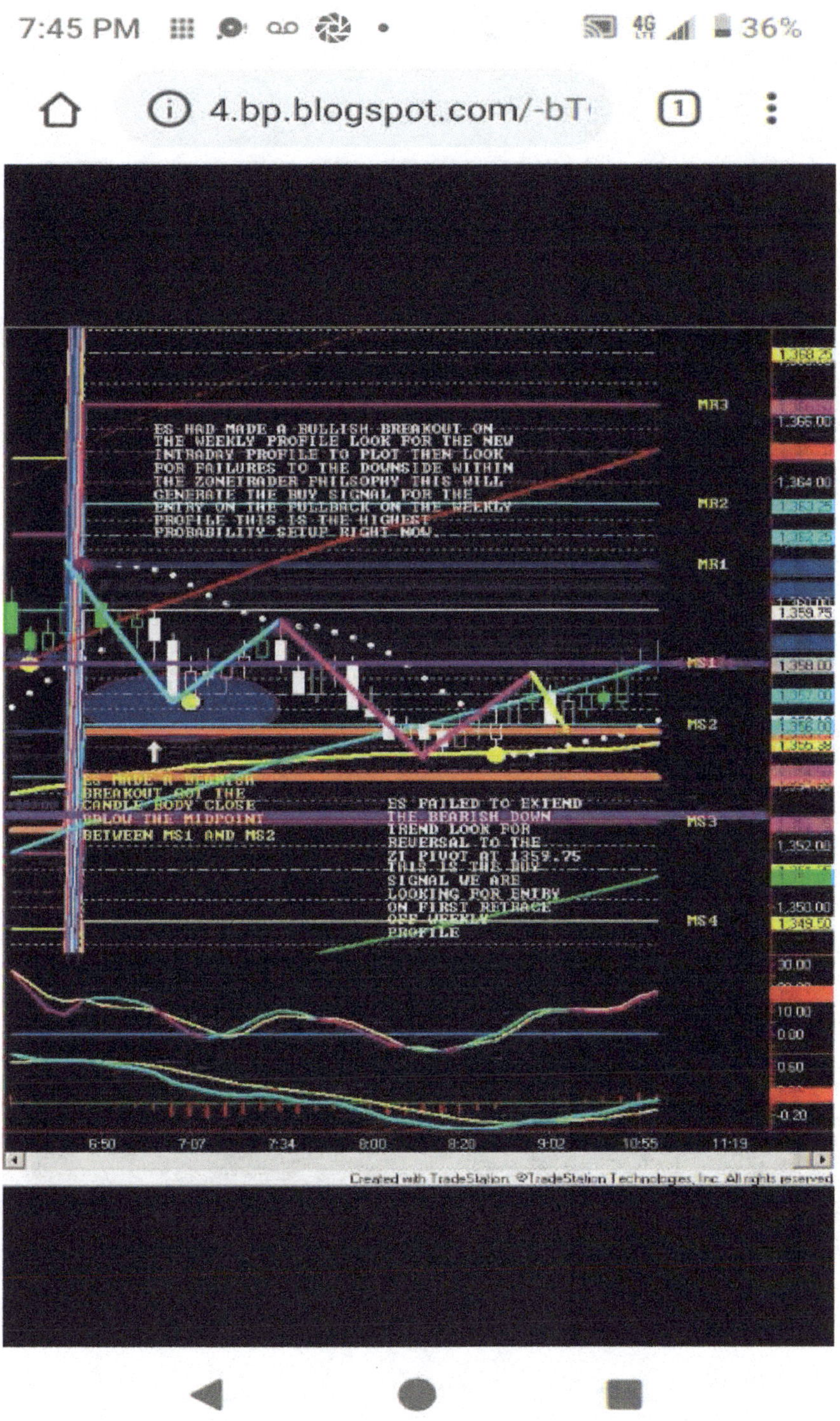

7:45 PM
36%
4.bp.blogspot.com/-bT
ES HAD MADE A BULLISH BREAKOUT ON
THE WEEKLY PROFILE LOOK FOR THE NEW
INTRADAY PROFILE TO PLOT THEN LOOK
FOR FAILURES TO THE DOWNSIDE WITHIN
THE ZONETRADER PHILSOPHY THIS WILL
GENERATE THE BUY SIGNAL FOR THE
ENTRY ON THE PULLBACK ON THE WEEKLY
PROFILE THIS IS THE HIGHEST
PROBABILITY SETUP RIGHT NOW.
MR3
MR2
MR1
MS1
MS2
MS3
MS4
CANDLE BODY CLOSE
BETWEEN MS1 AND MS2
ES FAILED TO EXTEND
THE BEARISH DOWN
TREND LOOK FOR
REVERSAL TO THE
ZI PIVOT AT 1359.75
SIGNAL WE ARE
LOOKING FOR ENTRY
ON FIRST RETRACE
PROFILE
1,366.00
1,364.00
1,359.75
1,358.00
1,352.00
1,350.00
1,349.50
30.00
10.00
0.00
0.60
-0.20
6:50
7:07
7:34
8:00
8:20
9:02
10:55
11:19
Created with TradeStation ©TradeStation Technologies, Inc. All rights reserved

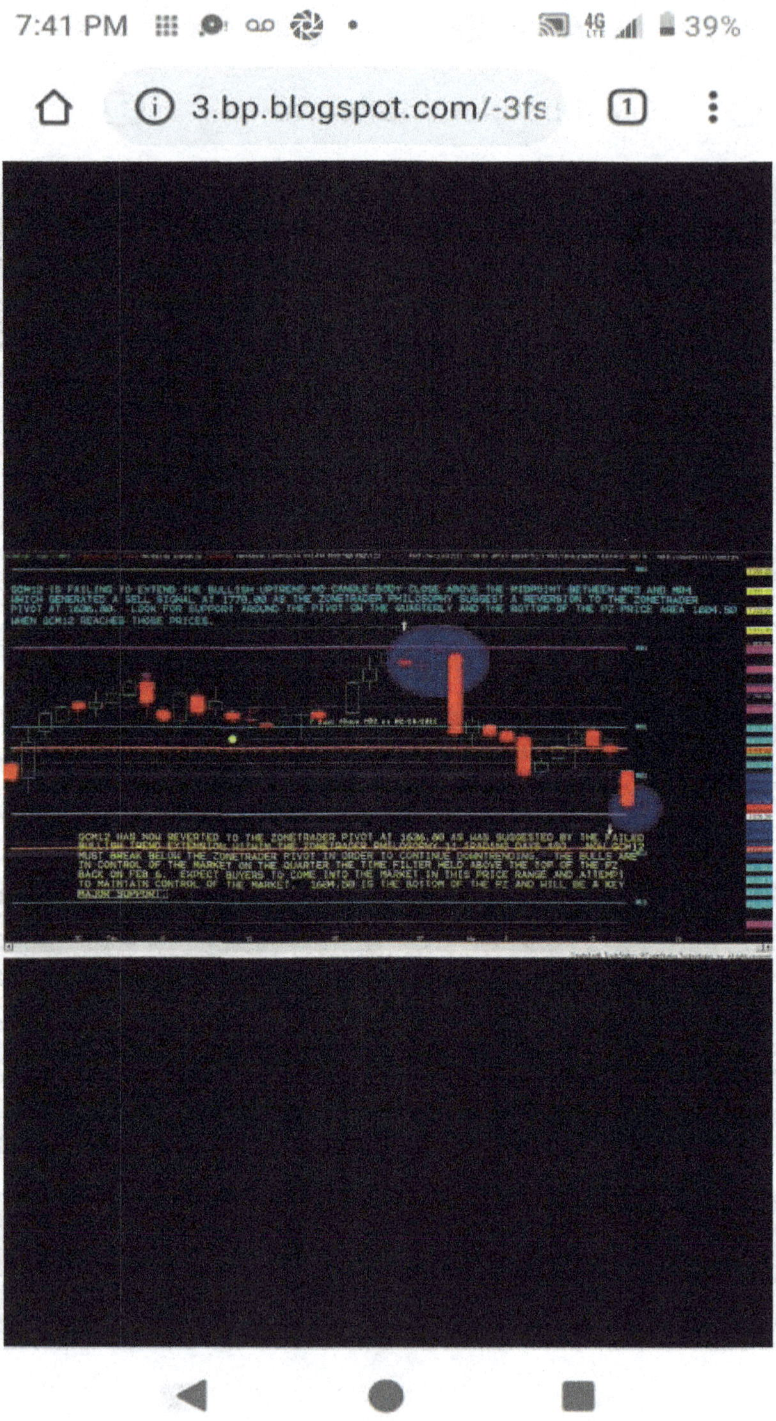
7:41 PM
39%
3.bp.blogspot.com/-3fs
GCM12 IS FAILING TO EXTEND THE BULLISH UPTREND NO CANDLE BODY CLOSE ABOVE THE MIDPOINT BETWEEN MR3 AND MR4 WHICH GENERATED A SELL SIGNAL AT 1770.80 AS THE ZONETRADER PHILOSOPHY SUGGEST A REVERSION TO THE ZONETRADER PIVOT AT 1636.80. LOOK FOR SUPPORT AROUND THE PIVOT ON THE QUARTERLY AND THE BOTTOM OF THE PZ PRICE AREA 1604.50 WHEN GCM12 REACHES THOSE PRICES.
MUST BREAK BELOW THE ZONETRADER PIVOT IN ORDER TO CONTINUE DOWNTRENDING. THE BULLS ARE IN CONTROL OF THE MARKET ON THE QUARTER THE TIME FILTER HELD ABOVE THE TOP OF THE PZ BACK ON FEB 6. EXPECT BUYERS TO COME INTO THE MARKET IN THIS PRICE RANGE AND ATTEMPT TO MAINTAIN CONTROL OF THE MARKET.
MAJOR SUPPORT.

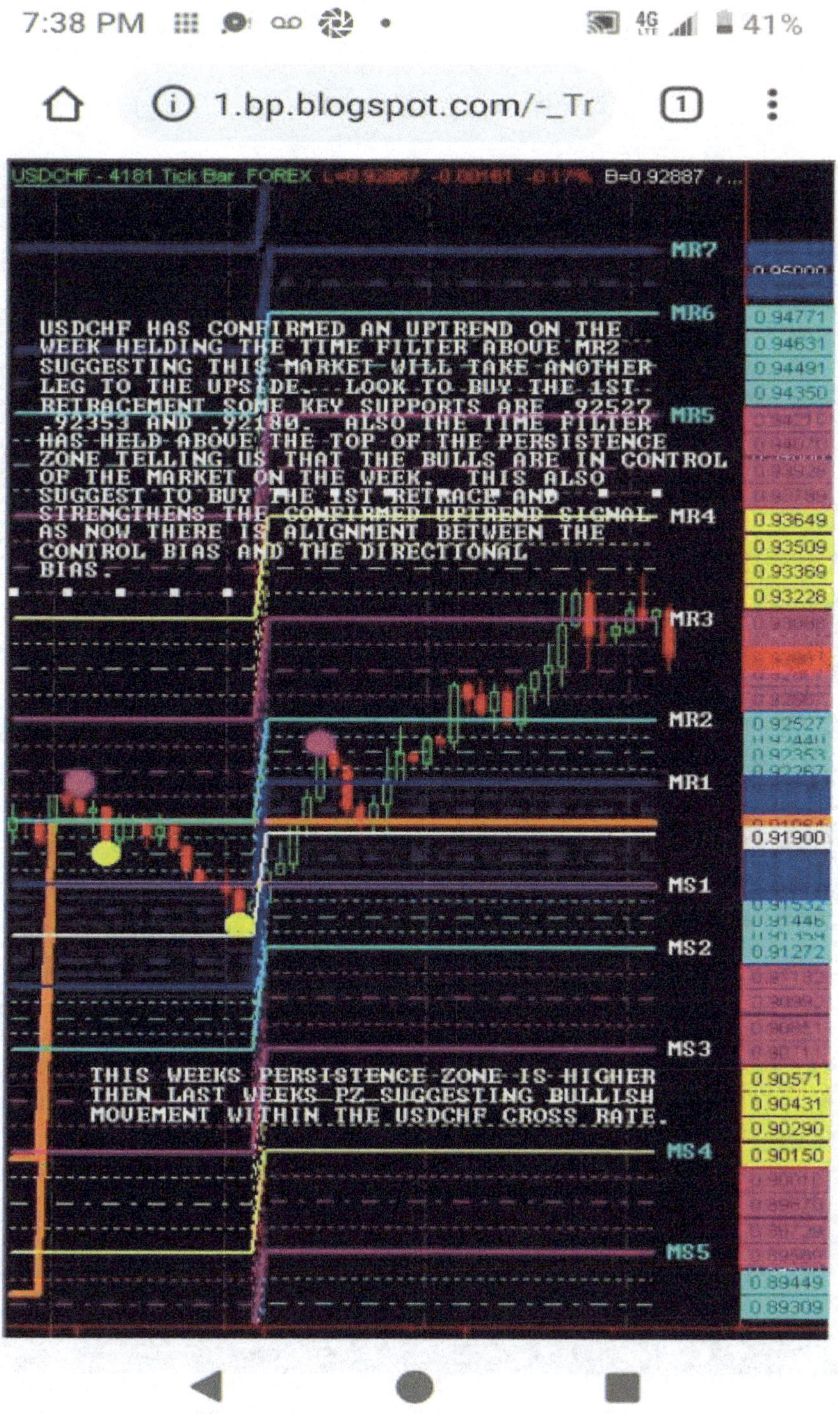
7:38 PM
41%
1.bp.blogspot.com/-_Tr
USDCHF - 4181 Tick Bar FOREX
B=0.92887
MR7
MR6
MR5
MR4
MR3
MR2
MR1
MS1
MS2
MS3
MS4
MS5
USDCHF HAS CONFIRMED AN UPTREND ON THE WEEK HELDING THE TIME FILTER ABOVE MR2 SUGGESTING THIS MARKET WILL TAKE ANOTHER LEG TO THE UPSIDE. LOOK TO BUY THE 1ST RETRACEMENT SOME KEY SUPPORTS ARE .92527 .92353 AND .92180. ALSO THE TIME FILTER HAS HELD ABOVE THE TOP OF THE PERSISTENCE ZONE TELLING US THAT THE BULLS ARE IN CONTROL OF THE MARKET ON THE WEEK. THIS ALSO SUGGEST TO BUY THE 1ST RETRACE AND STRENGTHENS THE CONFIRMED UPTREND SIGNAL AS NOW THERE IS ALIGNMENT BETWEEN THE CONTROL BIAS AND THE DIRECTIONAL BIAS.
THIS WEEKS PERSISTENCE ZONE IS HIGHER THEN LAST WEEKS PZ SUGGESTING BULLISH MOVEMENT WITHIN THE USDCHF CROSS RATE.
0.94771
0.94631
0.94491
0.94350
0.93649
0.93509
0.93369
0.93228
0.92527
0.92353
0.91900
0.91446
0.91272
0.90571
0.90431
0.90290
0.90150
0.89449
0.89309

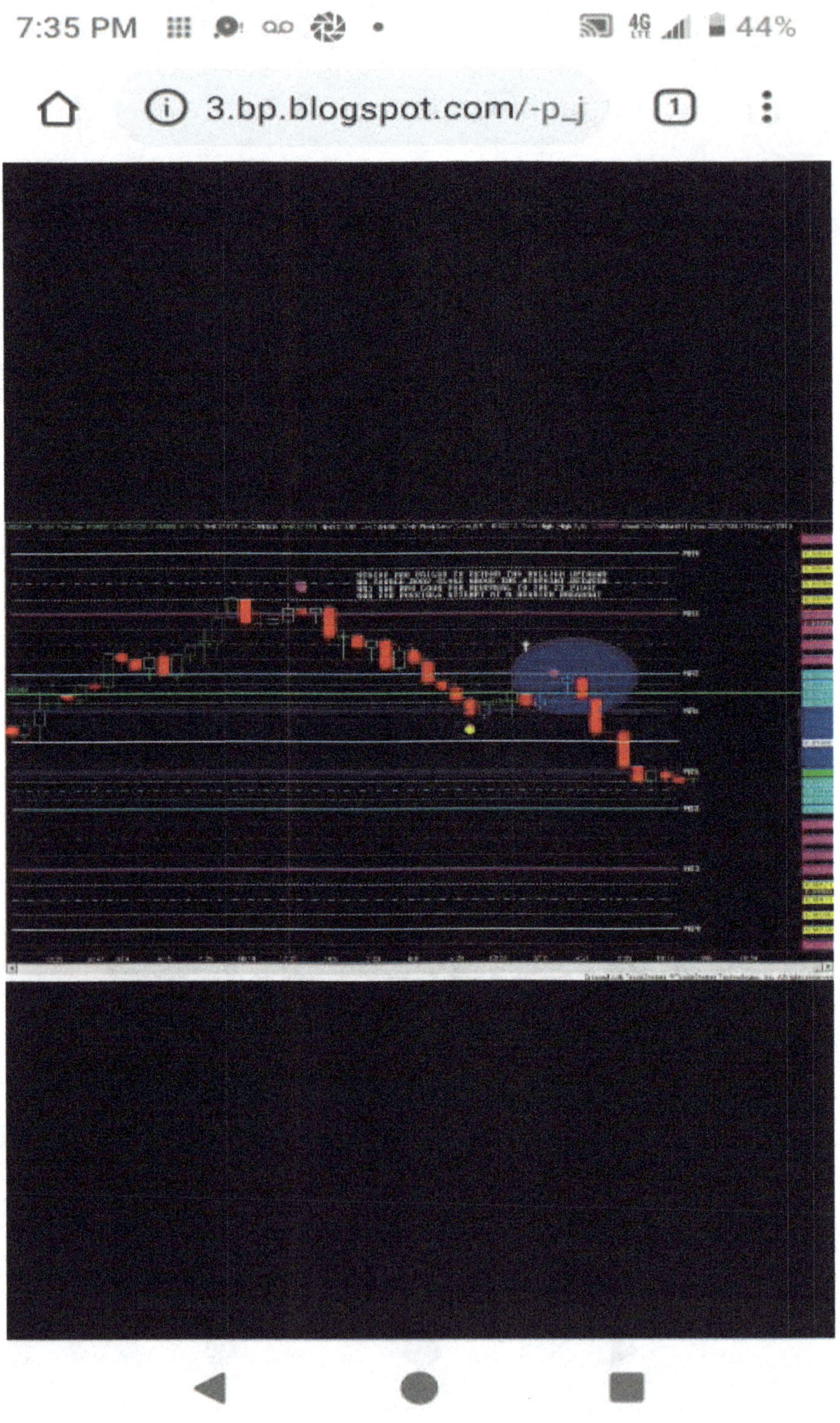
7:35 PM
44%
3.bp.blogspot.com/-p_j

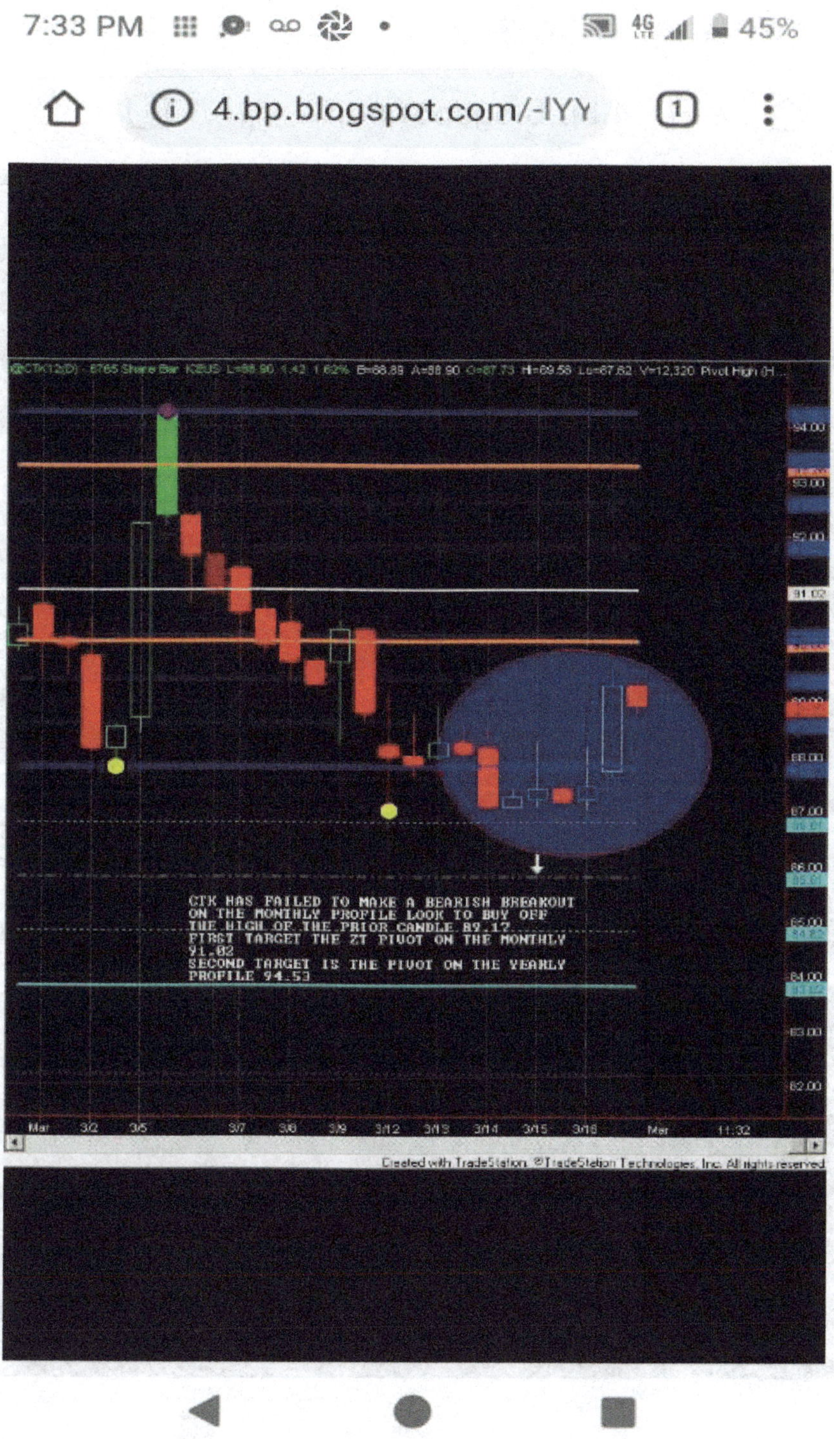
7:33 PM
45%
4.bp.blogspot.com/-lYY
CTK HAS FAILED TO MAKE A BEARISH BREAKOUT
ON THE MONTHLY PROFILE LOOK TO BUY OFF
THE HIGH OF THE PRIOR CANDLE 89.17
FIRST TARGET THE ZT PIVOT ON THE MONTHLY
91.02
SECOND TARGET IS THE PIVOT ON THE YEARLY
PROFILE 94.53
94.00
93.00
92.00
91.02
88.00
87.00
86.00
85.00
84.00
83.00
82.00
Mar
3/2
3/5
3/7
3/8
3/9
3/12
3/13
3/14
3/15
3/16
Mar
11:32
Created with TradeStation. ©TradeStation Technologies, Inc. All rights reserved.

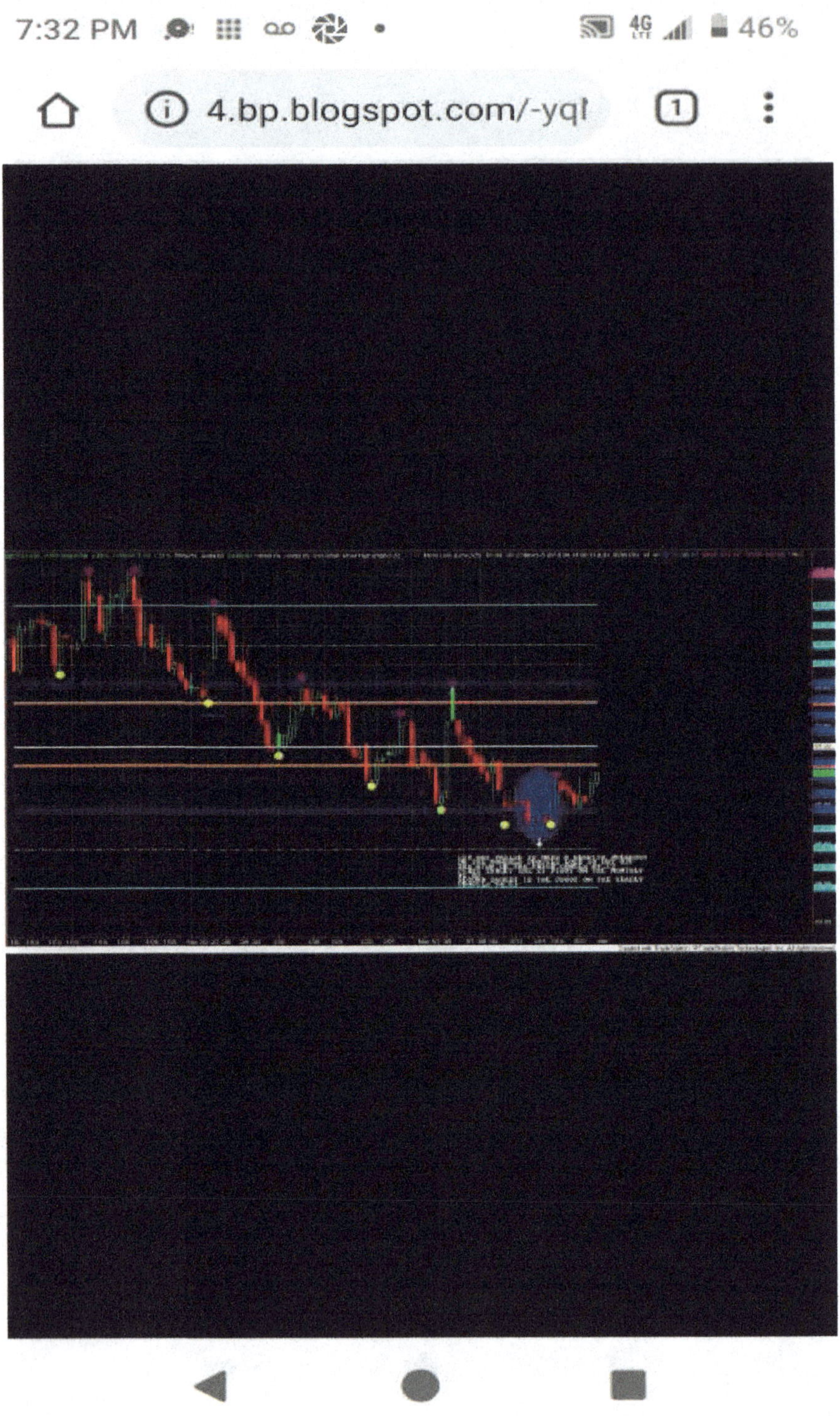
7:32 PM
4G
46%
4.bp.blogspot.com/-yql
1

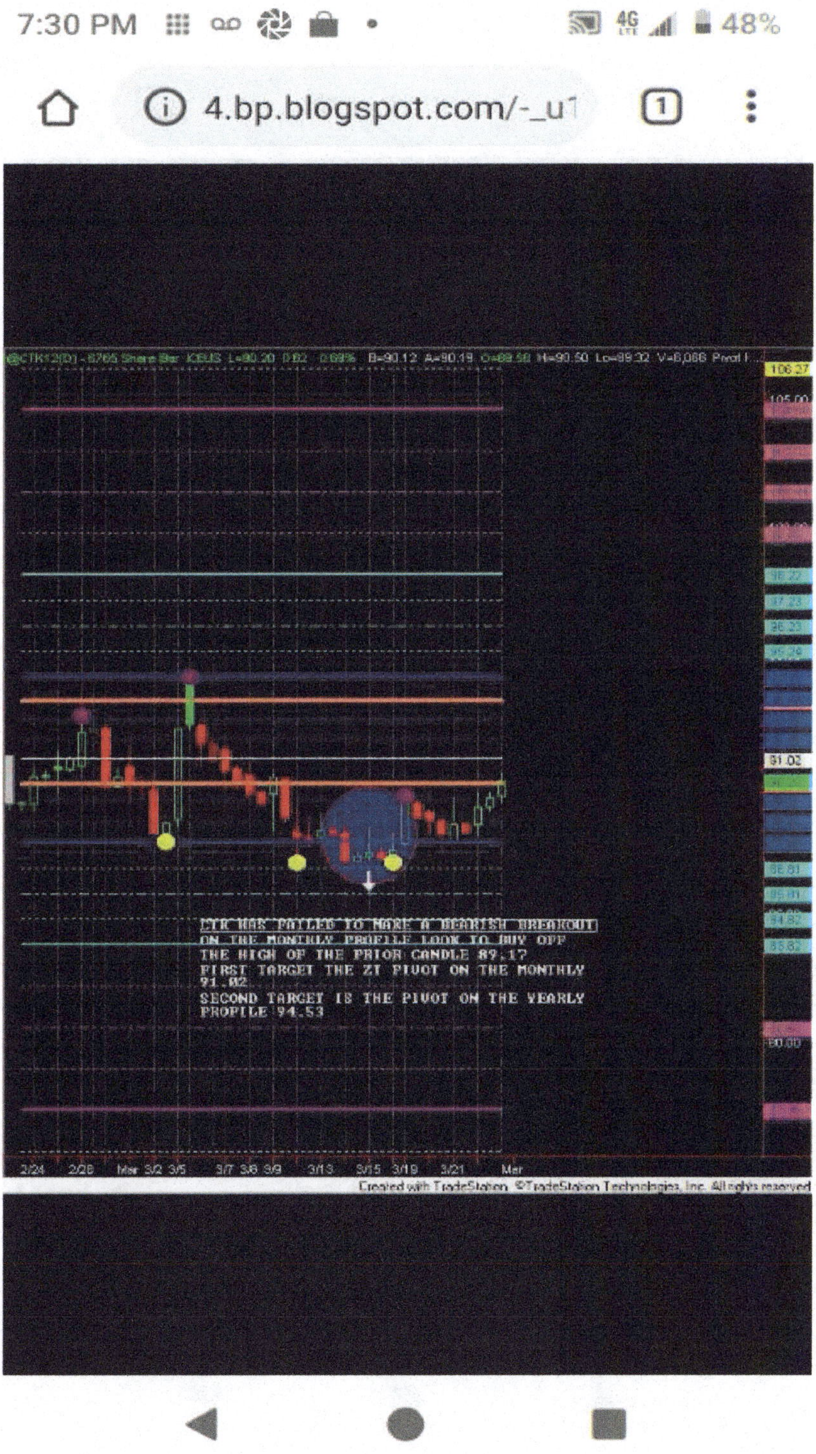
7:30 PM
48%
4.bp.blogspot.com/-_u1
CTR HAS FAILED TO MAKE A BEARISH BREAKOUT
ON THE MONTHLY PROFILE LOOK TO BUY OFF
THE HIGH OF THE PRIOR CANDLE 89.17
FIRST TARGET THE Z1 PIVOT ON THE MONTHLY
91.02
SECOND TARGET IS THE PIVOT ON THE YEARLY
PROFILE 94.53
Created with TradeStation. ©TradeStation Technologies, Inc. All rights reserved

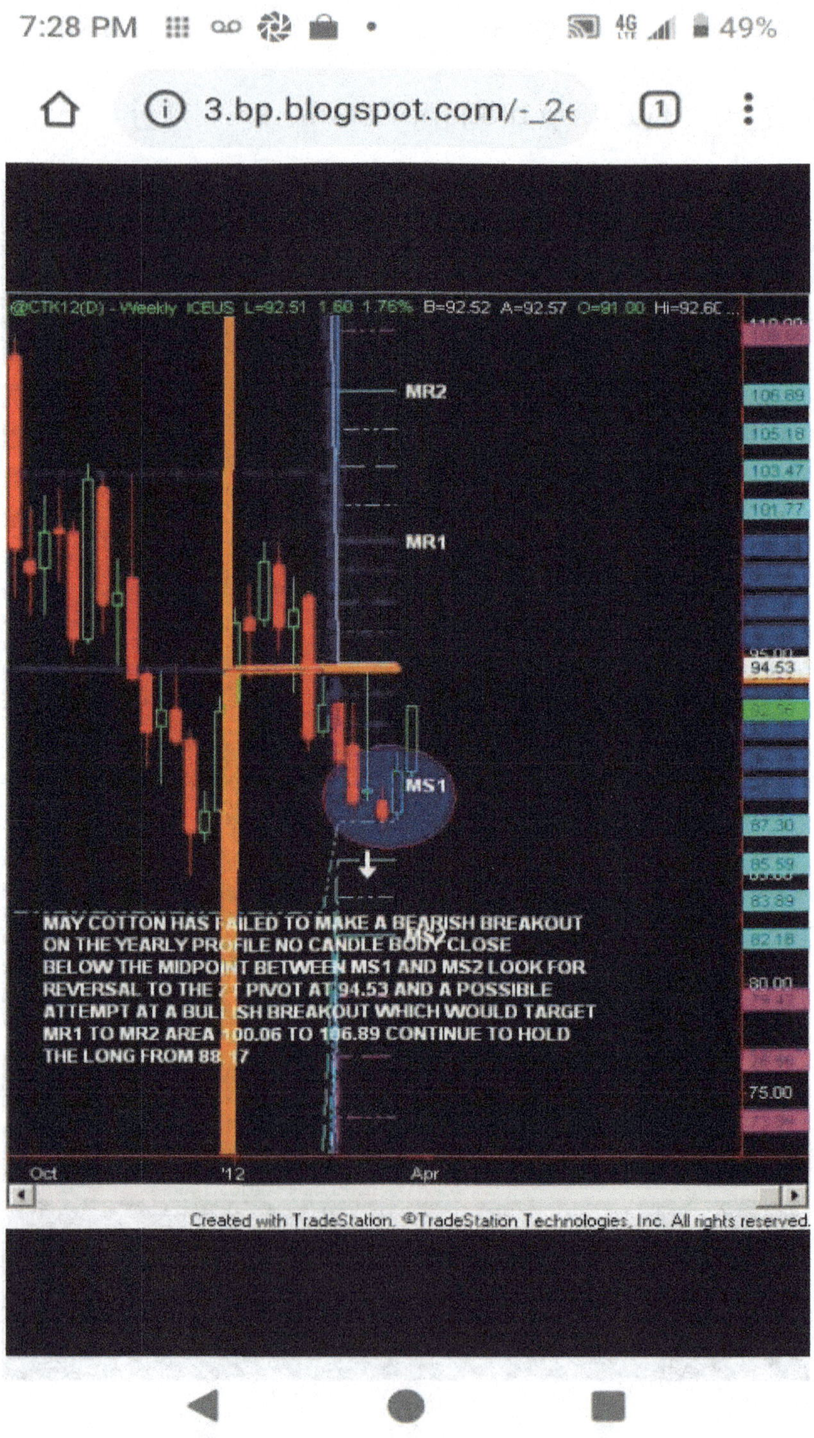
7:28 PM
49%
3.bp.blogspot.com/-_2
@CTK12(D) - Weekly ICEUS L=92.51 1.60 1.76% B=92.52 A=92.57 O=91.00
MR2
MR1
MS1
94.53
MAY COTTON HAS FAILED TO MAKE A BEARISH BREAKOUT ON THE YEARLY PROFILE NO CANDLE BODY CLOSE BELOW THE MIDPOINT BETWEEN MS1 AND MS2 LOOK FOR REVERSAL TO THE 7T PIVOT AT 94.53 AND A POSSIBLE ATTEMPT AT A BULLISH BREAKOUT WHICH WOULD TARGET MR1 TO MR2 AREA 100.06 TO 106.89 CONTINUE TO HOLD THE LONG FROM 88.17
80.00
75.00
Oct
'12
Apr
Created with TradeStation. ©TradeStation Technologies, Inc. All rights reserved.

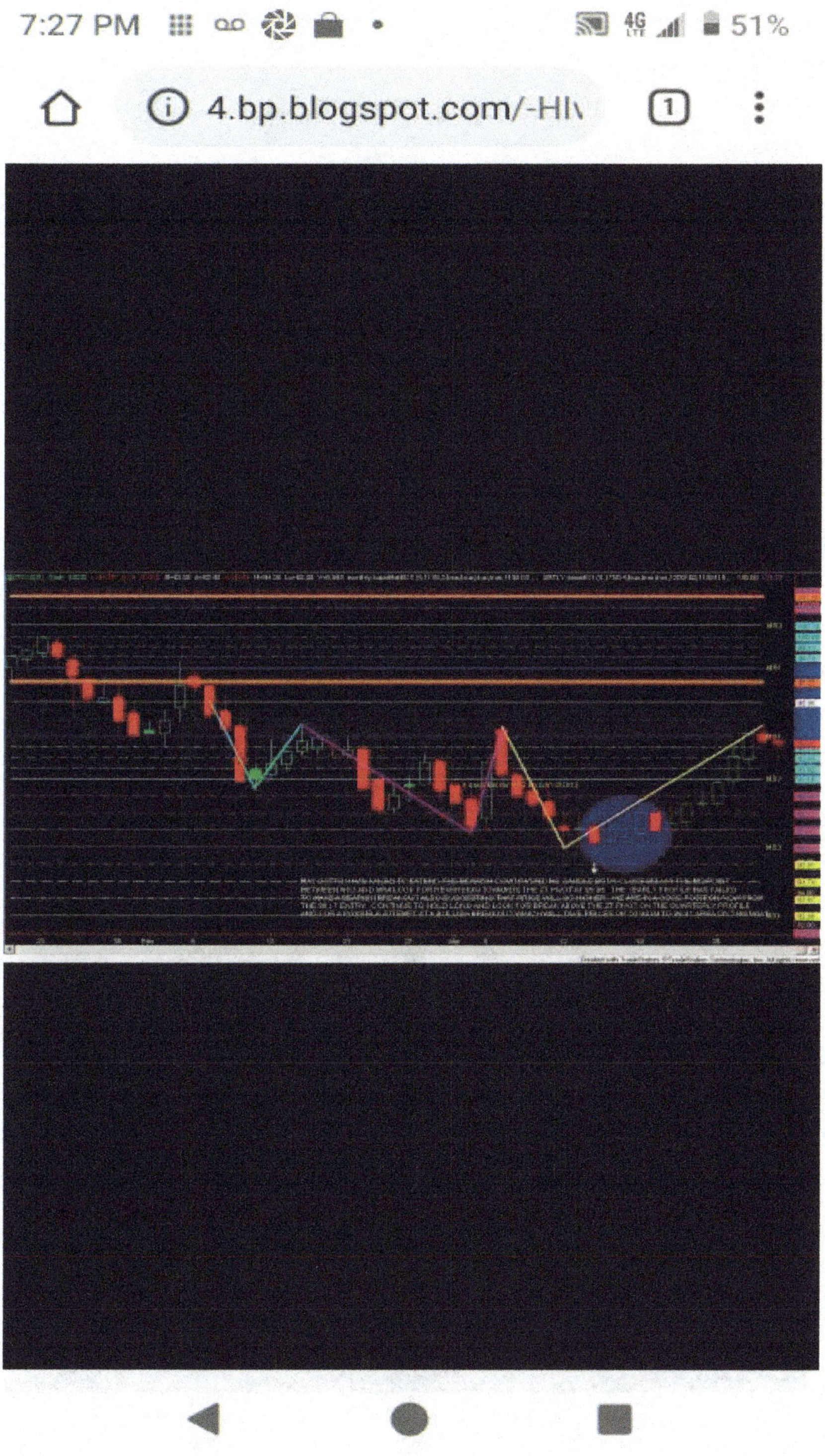
7:27 PM
4G
51%
4.bp.blogspot.com/-Hl

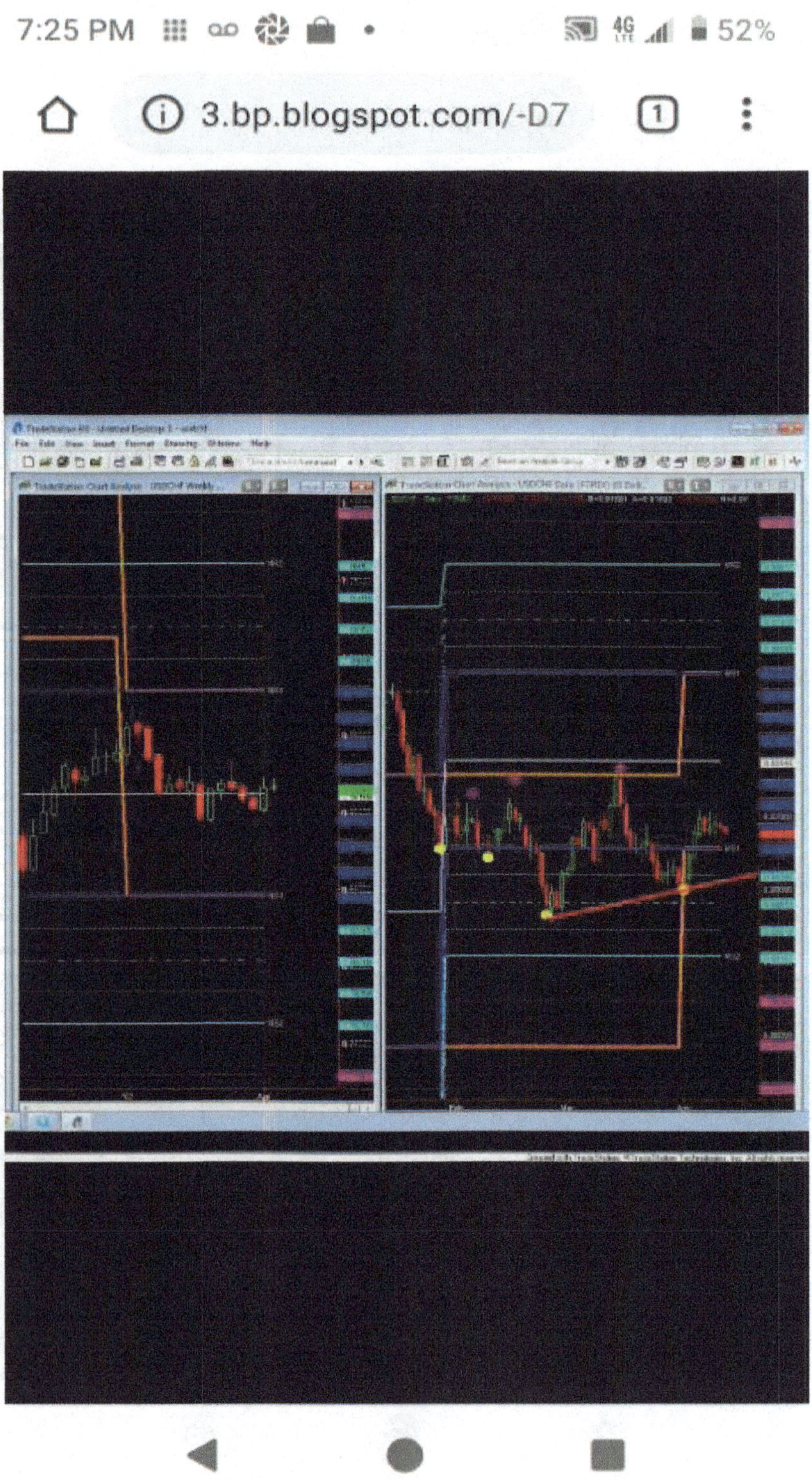
7:25 PM
52%
3.bp.blogspot.com/-D7

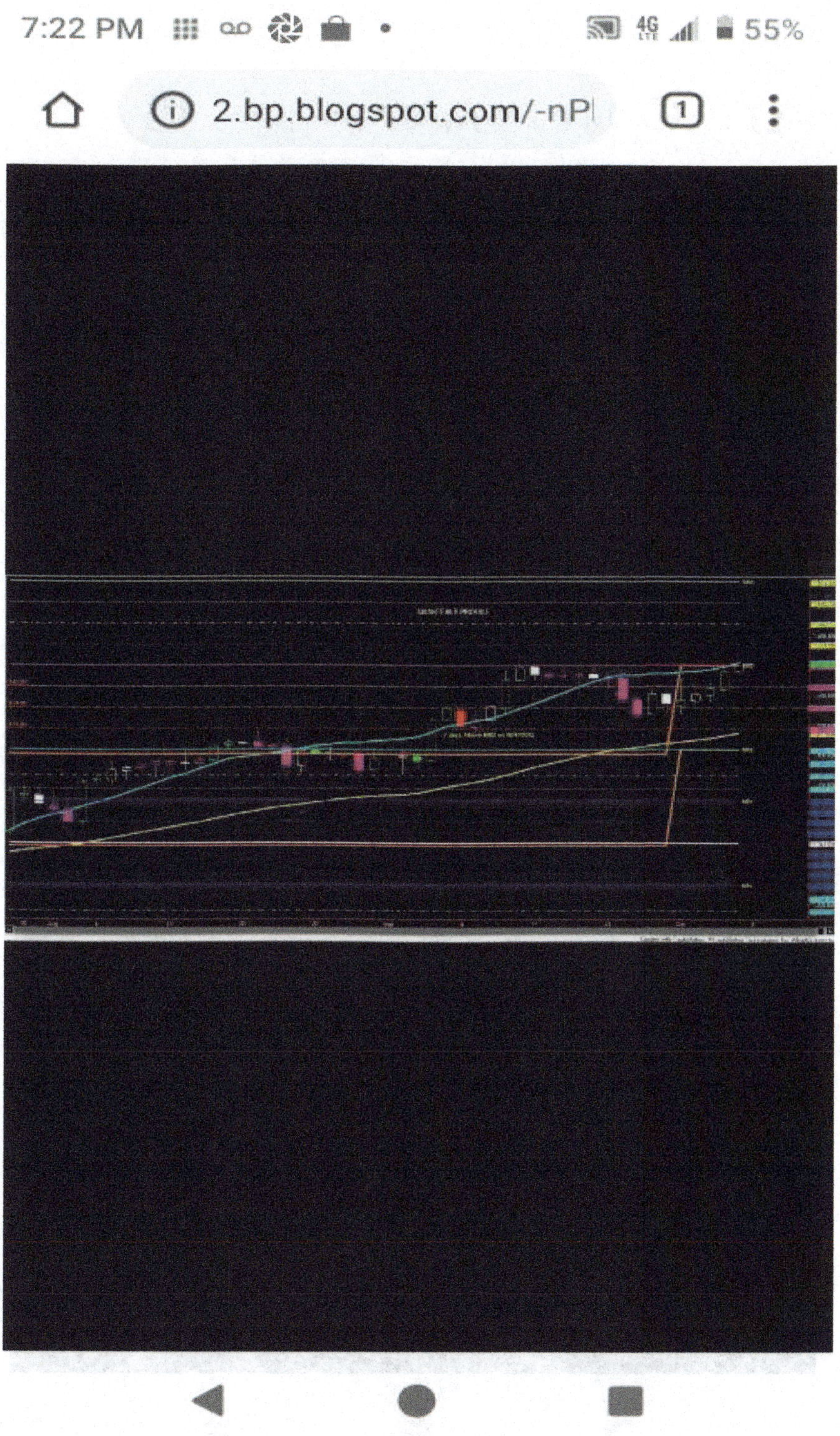
7:22 PM
4G
55%
2.bp.blogspot.com/-nPl
1

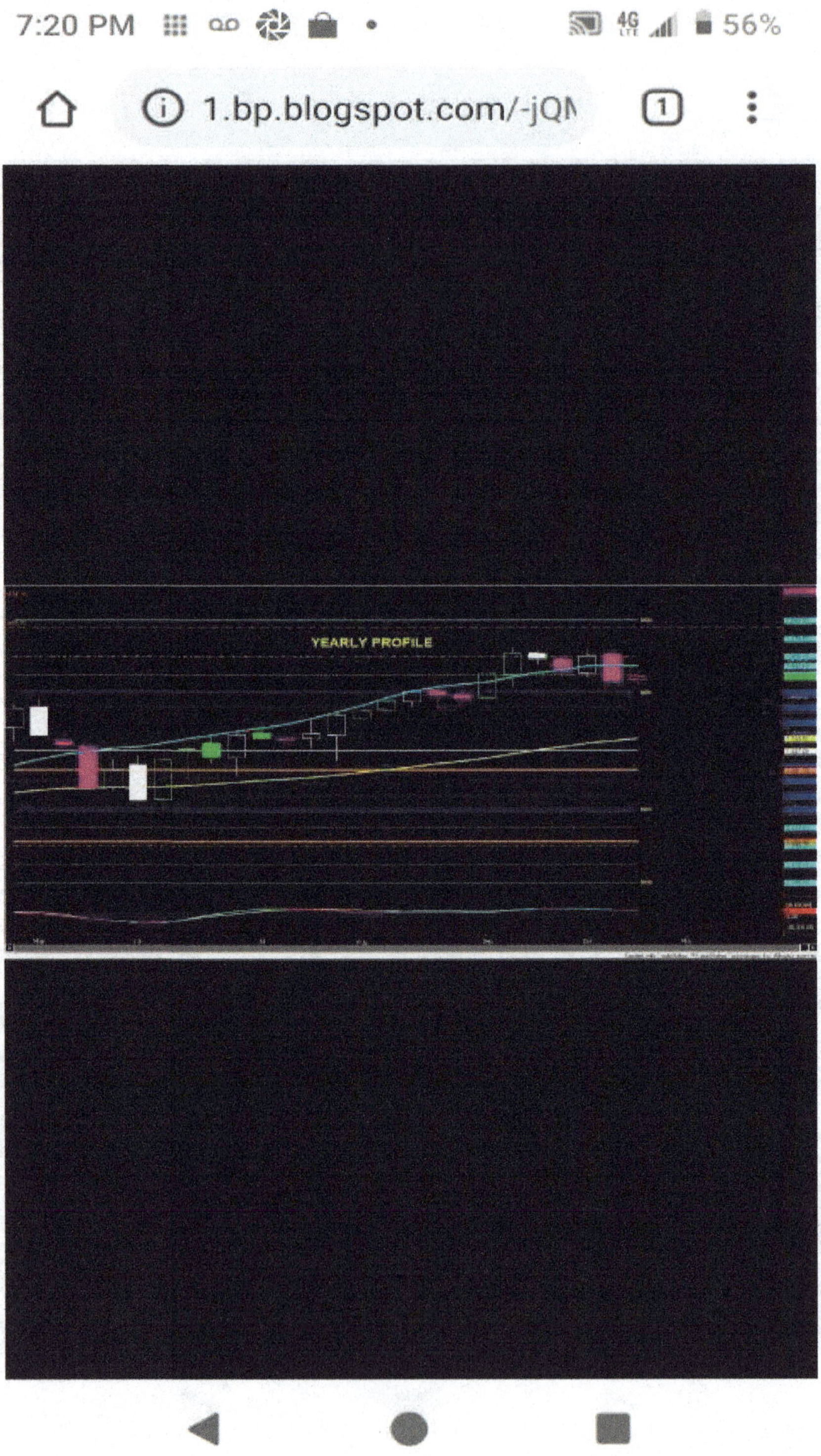
7:20 PM
56%
1.bp.blogspot.com/-jQM
YEARLY PROFILE

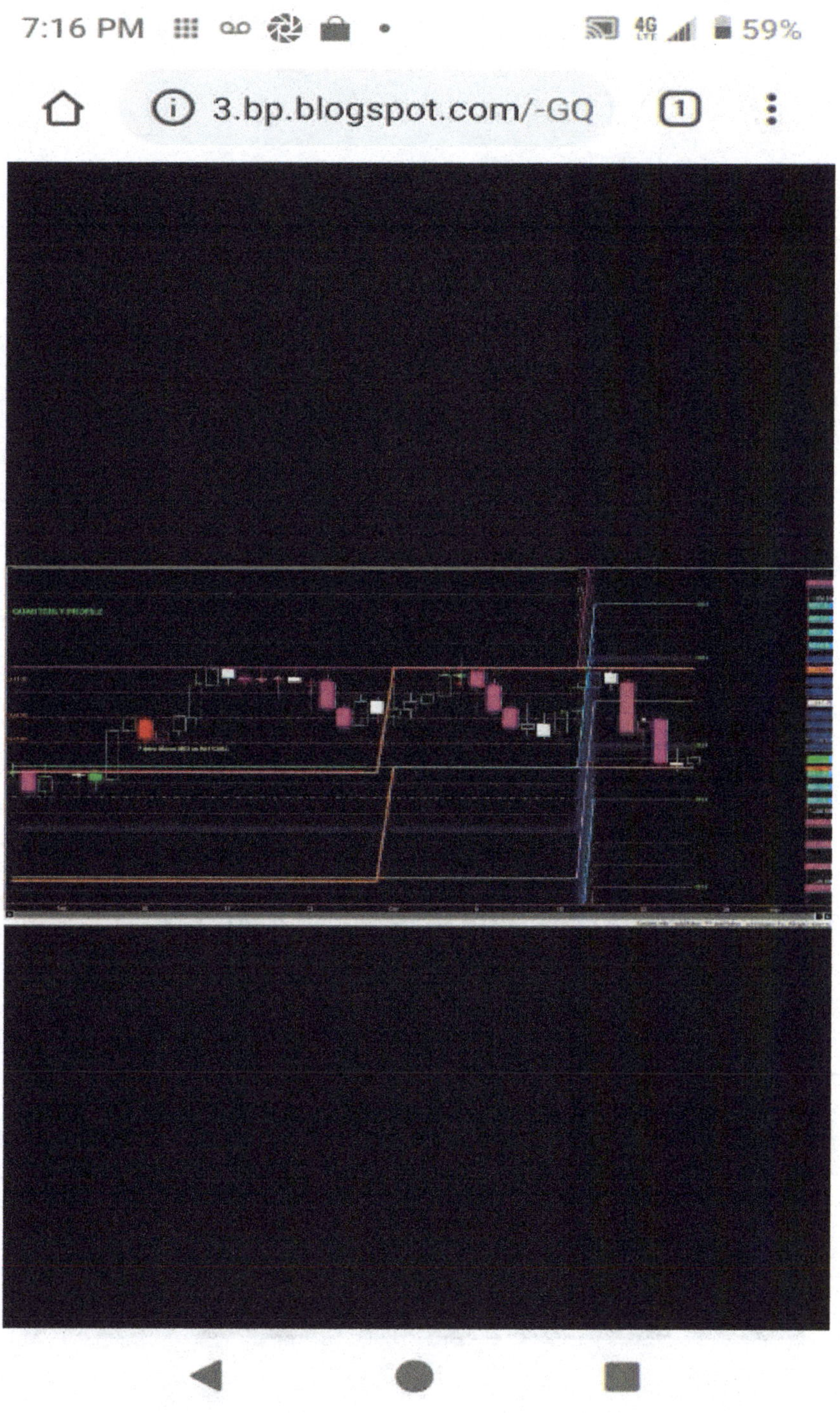
7:16 PM
4G
59%
3.bp.blogspot.com/-GQ
1

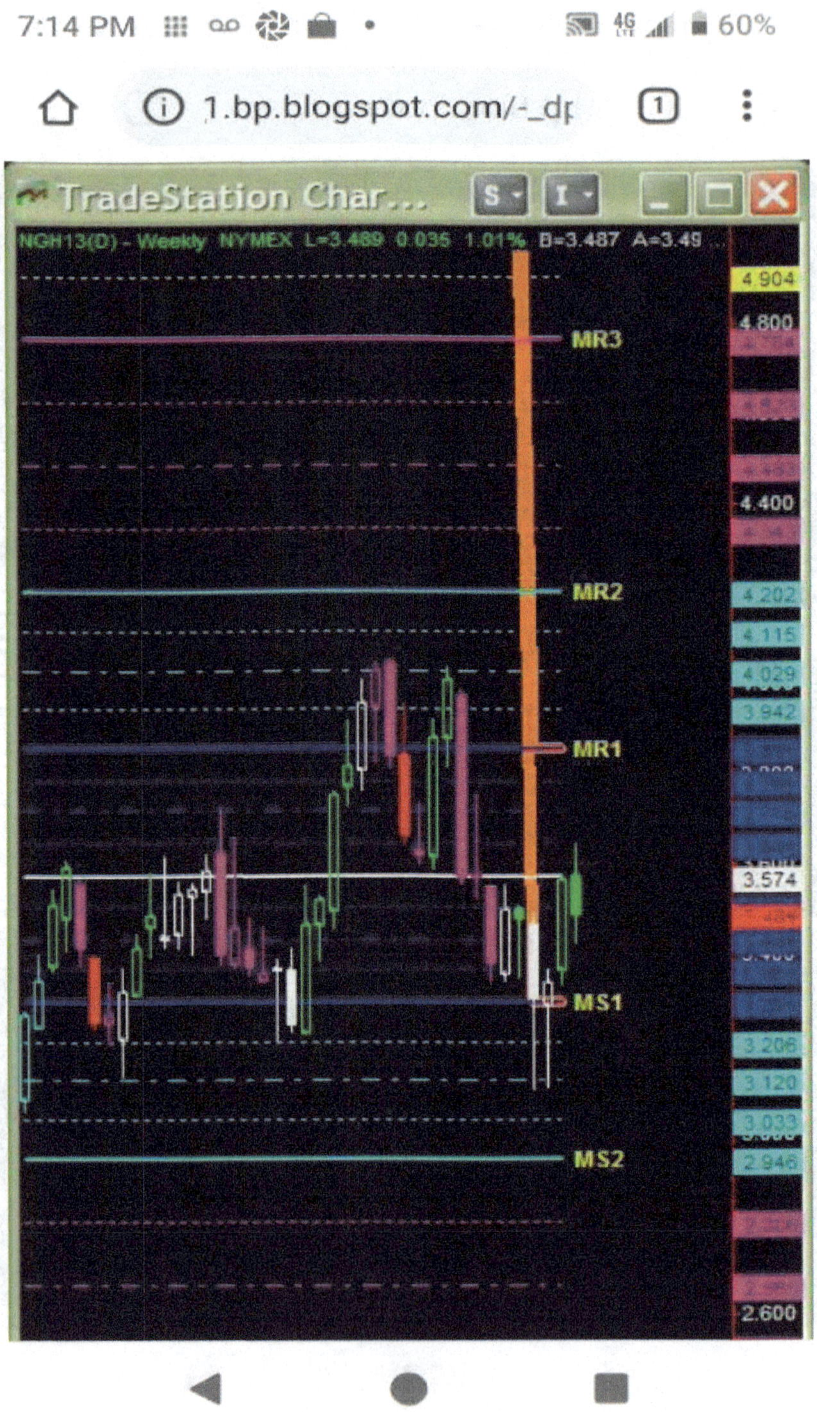
7:14 PM
60%
1.bp.blogspot.com/-_dp
TradeStation Char...
NGH13(D) - Weekly NYMEX L=3.489 0.035 1.01% B=3.487 A=3.49
4.904
4.800
MR3
4.400
MR2
4.202
4.115
4.029
3.942
MR1
3.574
MS1
3.206
3.120
3.033
MS2
2.946
2.600

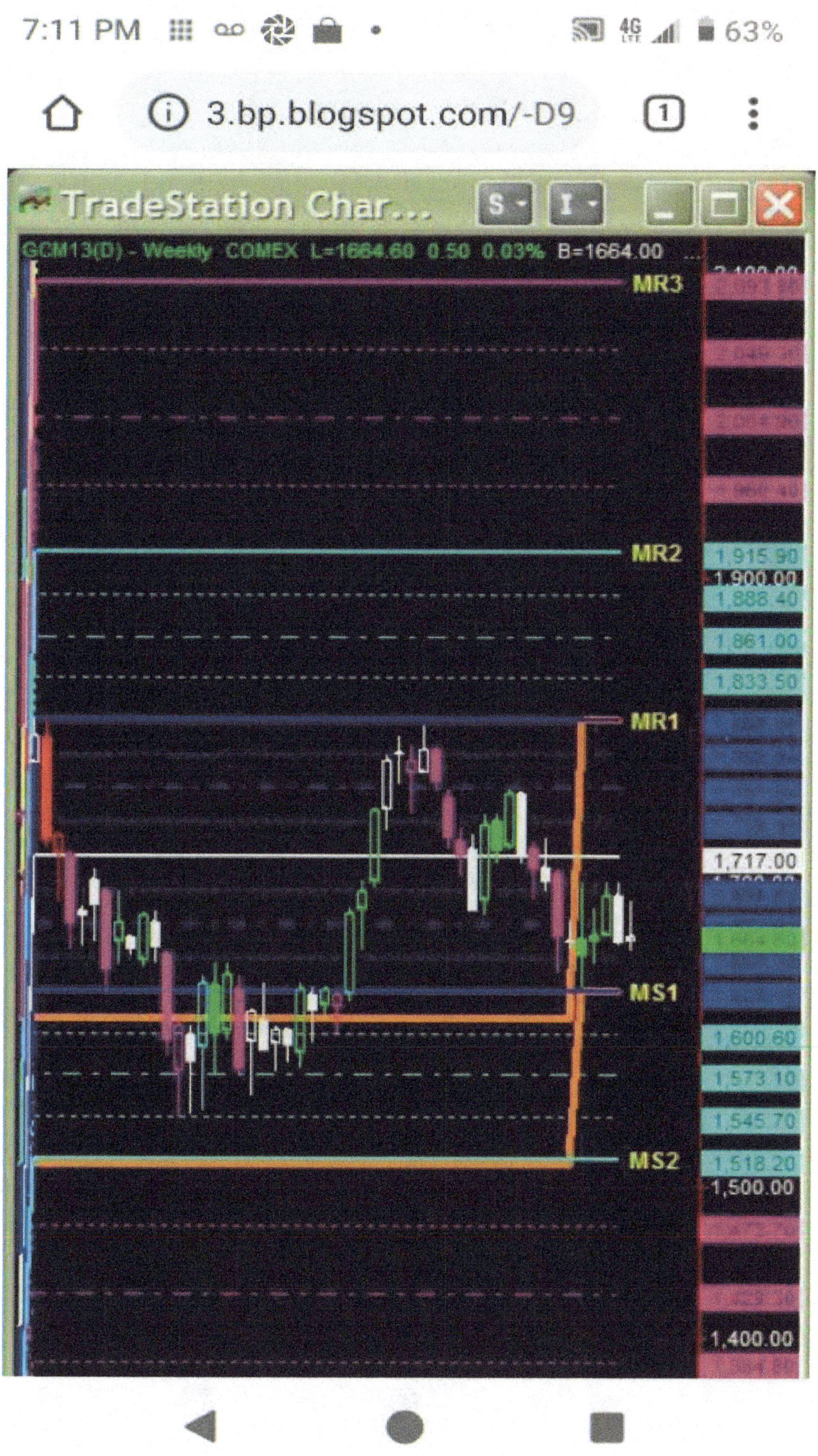
7:11 PM
63%
3.bp.blogspot.com/-D9
TradeStation Char...
GCM13(D) - Weekly COMEX L=1664.60 0.50 0.03% B=1664.00
MR3
MR2
1,915.90
1,900.00
1,888.40
1,861.00
1,833.50
MR1
1,717.00
MS1
1,600.60
1,573.10
1,545.70
MS2
1,518.20
1,500.00
1,400.00

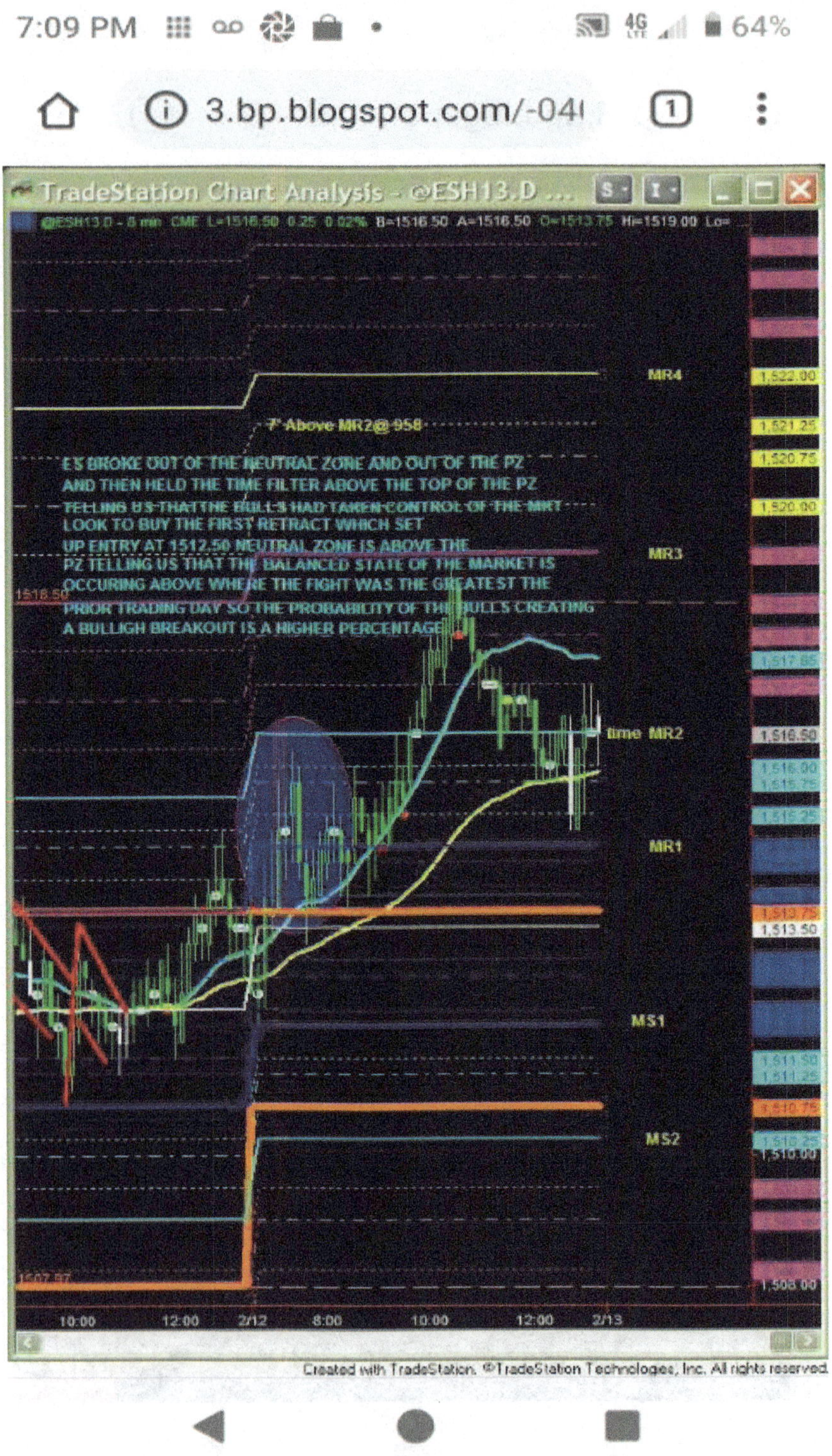
7:09 PM
64%
3.bp.blogspot.com/-04
TradeStation Chart Analysis - @ESH13.D ...
7' Above MR2@ 958
ES BROKE OUT OF THE NEUTRAL ZONE AND OUT OF THE PZ
AND THEN HELD THE TIME FILTER ABOVE THE TOP OF THE PZ
TELLING US THAT THE BULLS HAD TAKEN CONTROL OF THE MKT
LOOK TO BUY THE FIRST RETRACT WHICH SET
UP ENTRY AT 1512.50 NEUTRAL ZONE IS ABOVE THE
PZ TELLING US THAT THE BALANCED STATE OF THE MARKET IS
OCCURING ABOVE WHERE THE FIGHT WAS THE GREATEST THE
PRIOR TRADING DAY SO THE PROBABILITY OF THE BULLS CREATING
A BULLIGH BREAKOUT IS A HIGHER PERCENTAGE
MR4
MR3
time MR2
MR1
MS1
MS2
1,522.00
1,516.50
1,513.50
1,508.00
10:00
12:00
2/12
8:00
10:00
12:00
2/13
Created with TradeStation. ©TradeStation Technologies, Inc. All rights reserved.

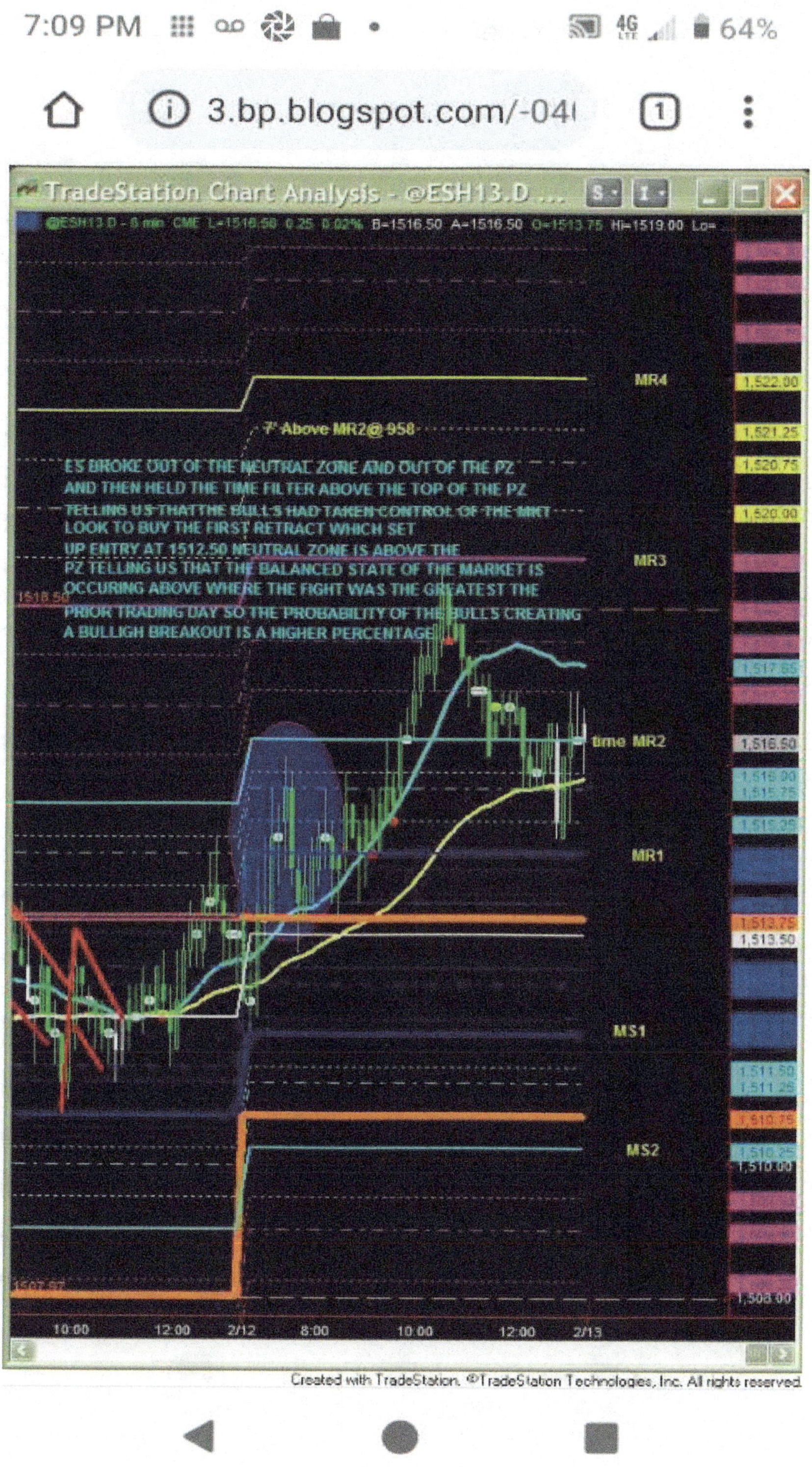
7:09 PM
64%
3.bp.blogspot.com/-04
TradeStation Chart Analysis - @ESH13.D ....
B=1516.50 A=1516.50
Hi=1519.00
MR4
1,522.00
7' Above MR2@ 958
1,521.25
ES BROKE OUT OF THE NEUTRAL ZONE AND OUT OF THE PZ
AND THEN HELD THE TIME FILTER ABOVE THE TOP OF THE PZ
TELLING US THATTHE BULLS HAD TAKEN CONTROL OF THE MKT
LOOK TO BUY THE FIRST RETRACT WHICH SET
UP ENTRY AT 1512.50 NEUTRAL ZONE IS ABOVE THE
PZ TELLING US THAT THE BALANCED STATE OF THE MARKET IS
OCCURING ABOVE WHERE THE FIGHT WAS THE GREATEST THE
PRIOR TRADING DAY SO THE PROBABILITY OF THE BULLS CREATING
A BULLIGH BREAKOUT IS A HIGHER PERCENTAGE
1,520.75
1,520.00
MR3
time MR2
1,516.50
MR1
1,513.50
MS1
MS2
1,510.00
1,508.00
10:00
12:00
2/12
8:00
10:00
12:00
2/13
Created with TradeStation. ©TradeStation Technologies, Inc. All rights reserved.

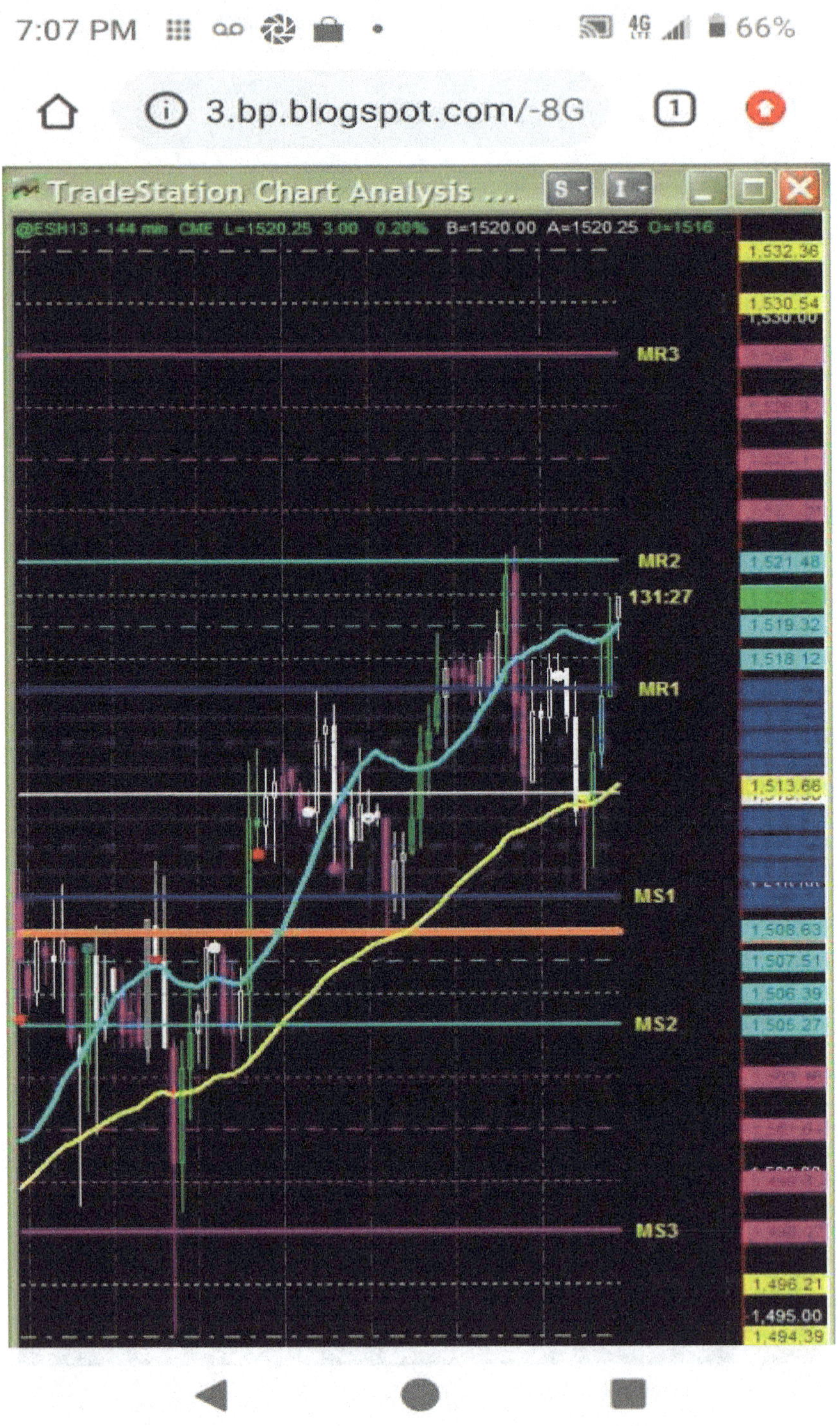
7:07 PM
66%
3.bp.blogspot.com/-8G
TradeStation Chart Analysis ...
@ESH13 - 144 min CME L=1520.25 3.00 0.20% B=1520.00 A=1520.25 O=1516
1,532.36
1,530.54
MR3
MR2
131:27
1,521.48
1,519.32
1,518.12
MR1
1,513.66
MS1
1,508.63
1,507.51
1,506.39
1,505.27
MS2
MS3
1,496.21
1,495.00
1,494.39

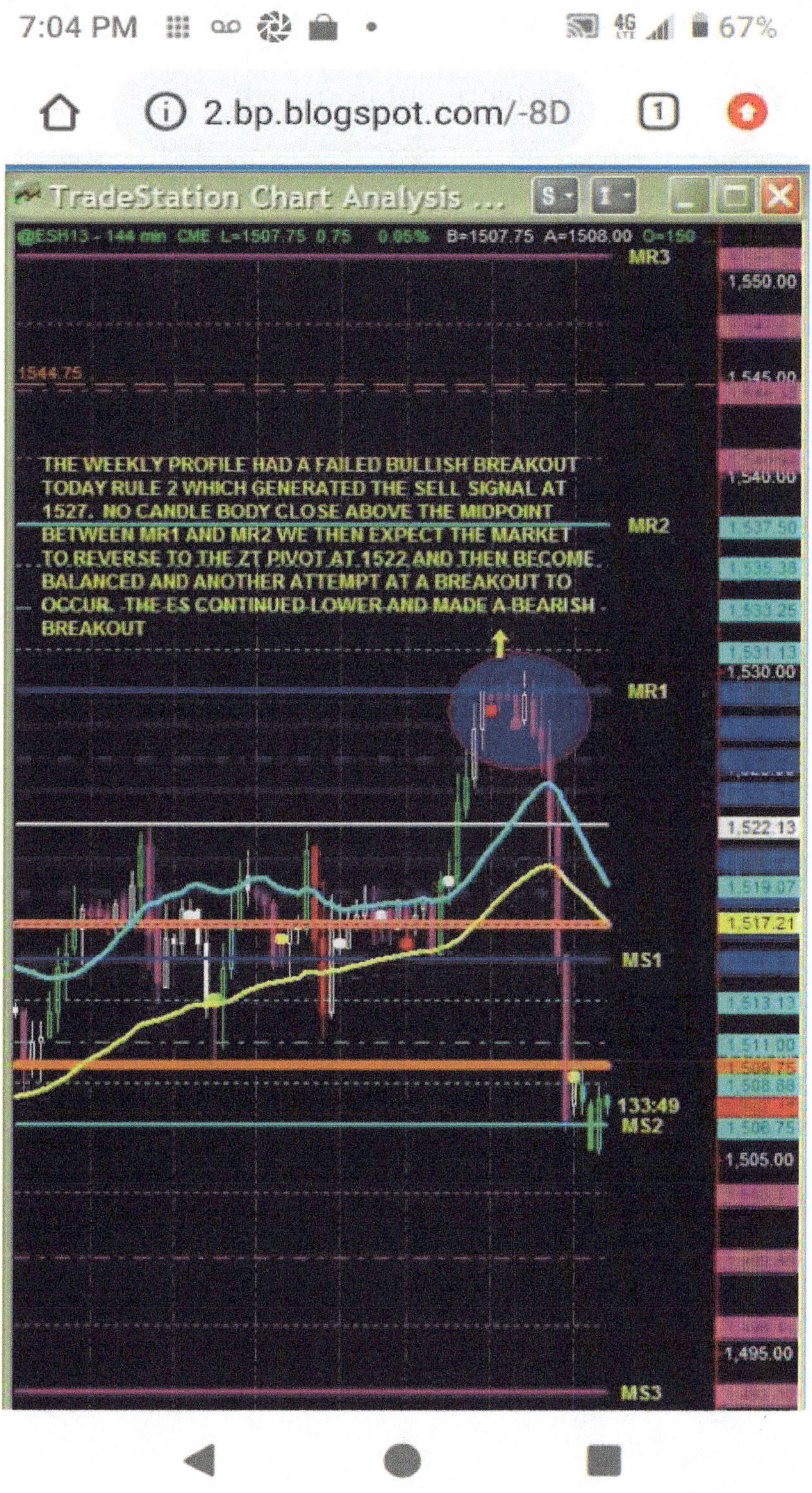
7:04 PM
67%
2.bp.blogspot.com/-8D
TradeStation Chart Analysis ...
@ESH13 - 144 min CME L=1507.75 0.75 0.05% B=1507.75 A=1508.00
MR3
1,550.00
1544.75
1,545.00
THE WEEKLY PROFILE HAD A FAILED BULLISH BREAKOUT TODAY RULE 2 WHICH GENERATED THE SELL SIGNAL AT 1527. NO CANDLE BODY CLOSE ABOVE THE MIDPOINT BETWEEN MR1 AND MR2 WE THEN EXPECT THE MARKET TO REVERSE TO THE ZT PIVOT AT 1522 AND THEN BECOME BALANCED AND ANOTHER ATTEMPT AT A BREAKOUT TO OCCUR. THE ES CONTINUED LOWER AND MADE A BEARISH BREAKOUT
1,540.00
MR2
1,530.00
MR1
1,522.13
1,517.21
MS1
133:49
MS2
1,505.00
1,495.00
MS3

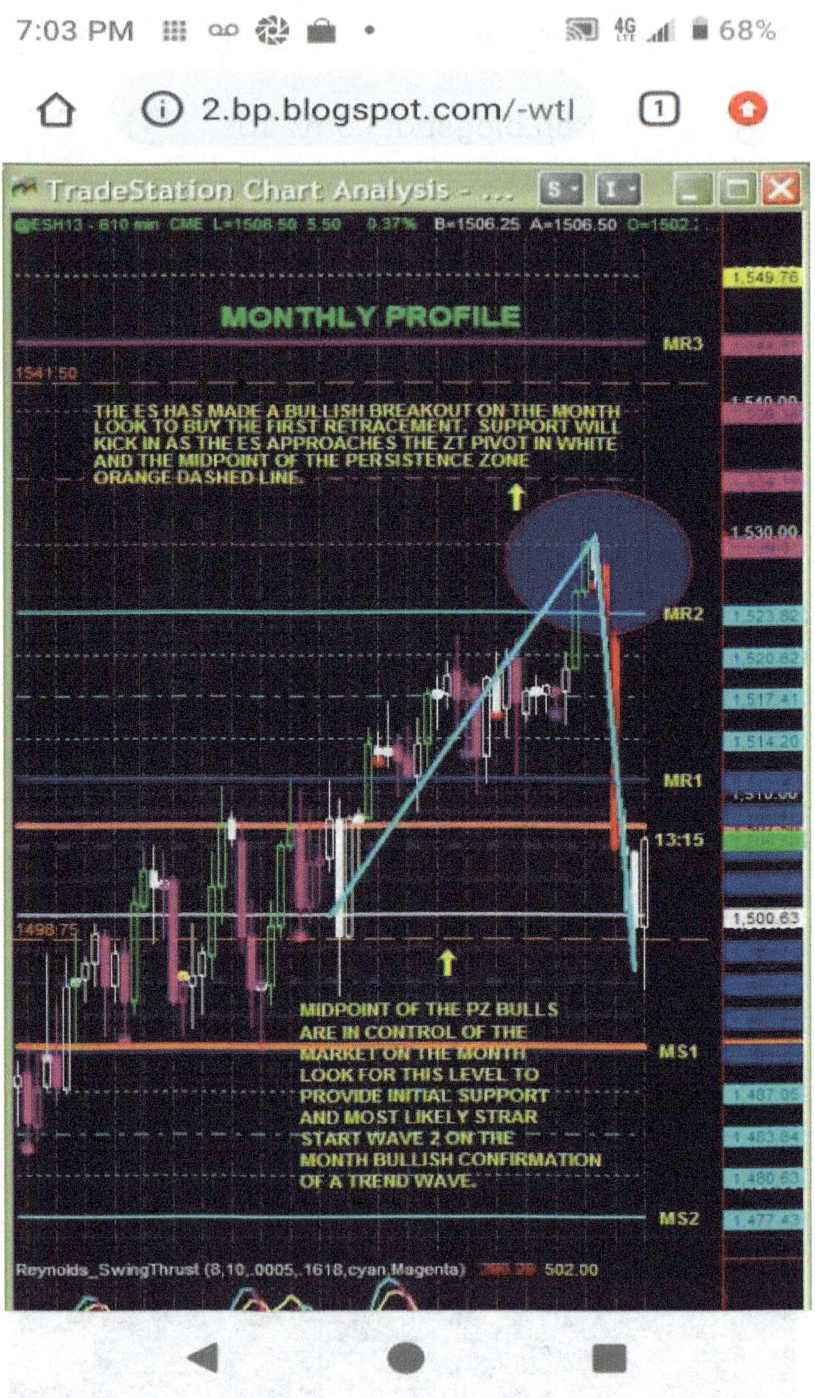
7:03 PM
68%
2.bp.blogspot.com/-wtl
TradeStation Chart Analysis - ...
@ESH13 - 610 min CME L=1506.50 5.50 0.37% B=1506.25 A=1506.50
MONTHLY PROFILE
MR3
1541.50
THE ES HAS MADE A BULLISH BREAKOUT ON THE MONTH LOOK TO BUY THE FIRST RETRACEMENT. SUPPORT WILL KICK IN AS THE ES APPROACHES THE ZT PIVOT IN WHITE AND THE MIDPOINT OF THE PERSISTENCE ZONE ORANGE DASHED LINE.
MR2
MR1
13:15
1498.75
MIDPOINT OF THE PZ BULLS ARE IN CONTROL OF THE MARKET ON THE MONTH LOOK FOR THIS LEVEL TO PROVIDE INITIAL SUPPORT AND MOST LIKELY STRAR START WAVE 2 ON THE MONTH BULLISH CONFIRMATION OF A TREND WAVE.
MS1
MS2
1,549.76
1,530.00
1,523.62
1,520.82
1,517.41
1,514.20
1,500.63
1,487.05
1,483.84
1,480.63
1,477.43
Reynolds_SwingThrust (8,10,.0005,.1618,cyan,Magenta) 502.00

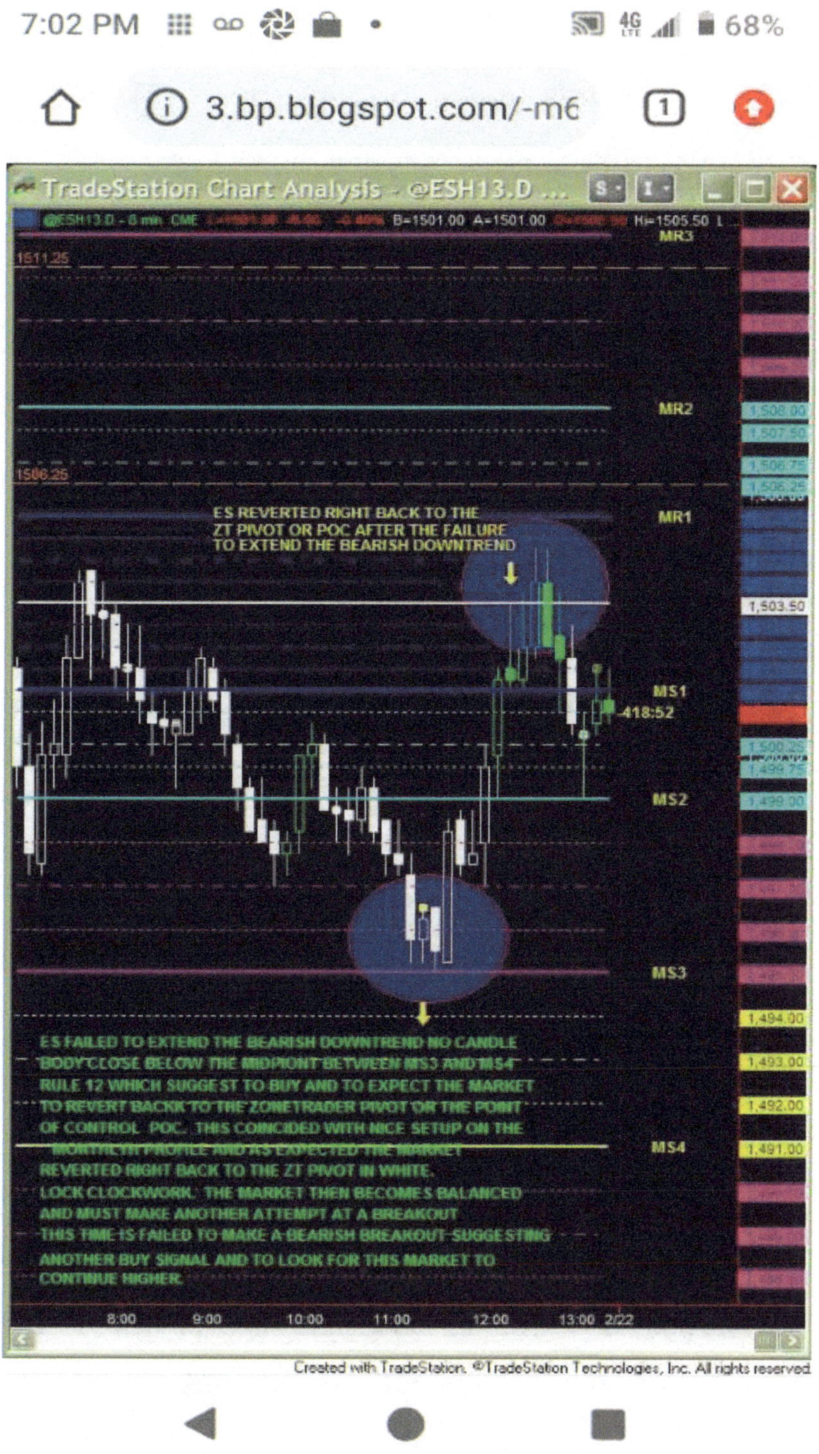
7:02 PM
68%
3.bp.blogspot.com/-m6
TradeStation Chart Analysis - @ESH13.D ...
B=1501.00 A=1501.00
H=1505.50
MR3
1511.25
MR2
1,508.00
1,507.50
1,506.75
1,506.25
1506.25
ES REVERTED RIGHT BACK TO THE
ZT PIVOT OR POC AFTER THE FAILURE
TO EXTEND THE BEARISH DOWNTREND
MR1
1,503.50
MS1
418:52
1,500.25
1,499.75
MS2
1,499.00
MS3
1,494.00
1,493.00
1,492.00
1,491.00
MS4
ES FAILED TO EXTEND THE BEARISH DOWNTREND NO CANDLE
BODY CLOSE BELOW THE MIDPIONT BETWEEN MS3 AND MS4
RULE 12 WHICH SUGGEST TO BUY AND TO EXPECT THE MARKET
TO REVERT BACKK TO THE ZONETRADER PIVOT OR THE POINT
OF CONTROL POC. THIS COINCIDED WITH NICE SETUP ON THE
REVERTED RIGHT BACK TO THE ZT PIVOT IN WHITE.
LOCK CLOCKWORK. THE MARKET THEN BECOMES BALANCED
AND MUST MAKE ANOTHER ATTEMPT AT A BREAKOUT
THIS TIME IS FAILED TO MAKE A BEARISH BREAKOUT SUGGESTING
ANOTHER BUY SIGNAL AND TO LOOK FOR THIS MARKET TO
CONTINUE HIGHER.
8:00
9:00
10:00
11:00
12:00
13:00 2/22
Created with TradeStation. ©TradeStation Technologies, Inc. All rights reserved.

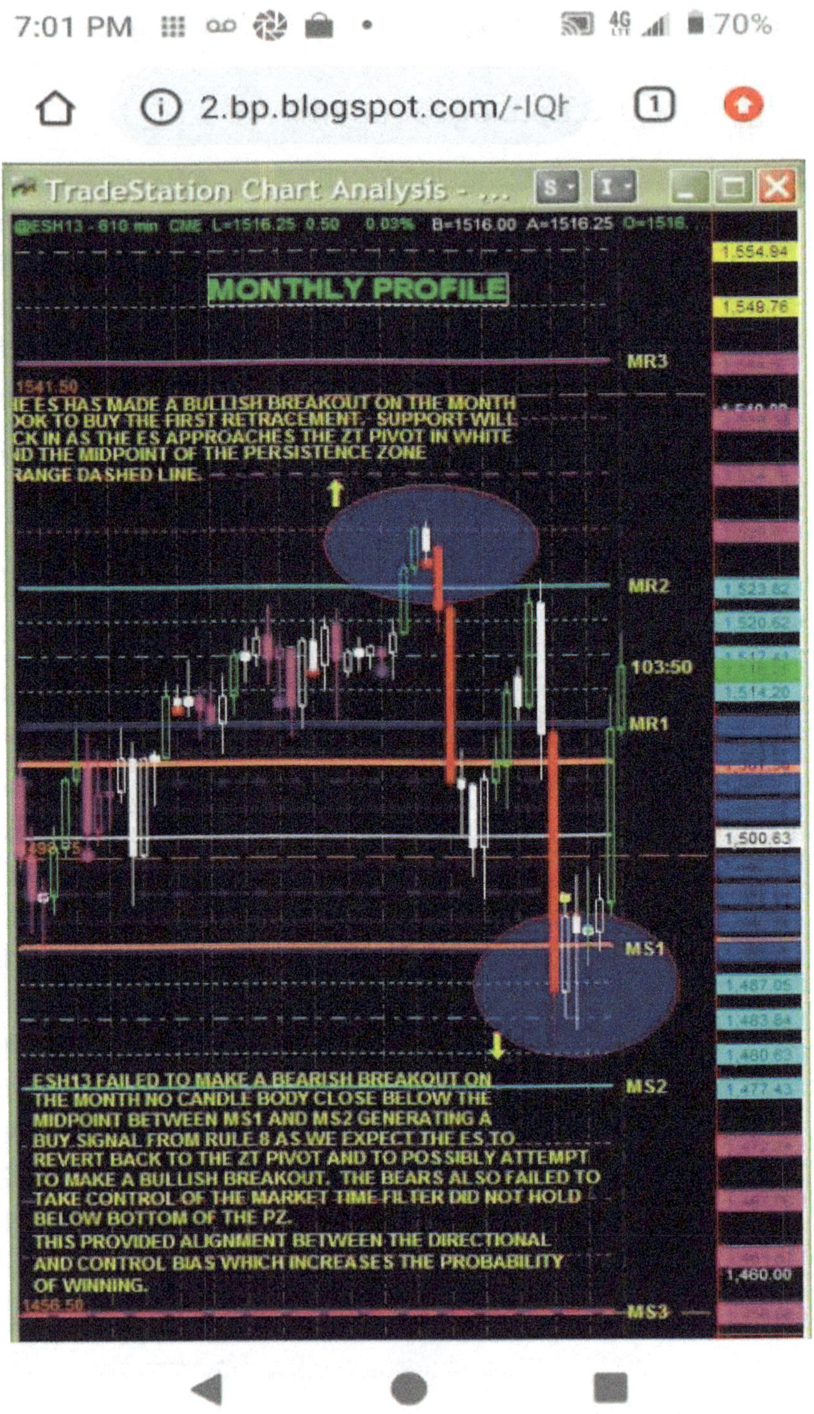
7:01 PM
70%
2.bp.blogspot.com/-IQI
TradeStation Chart Analysis - ...
@ESH13 - 610 min CME L=1516.25 0.50 0.03% B=1516.00 A=1516.25 O=1516
MONTHLY PROFILE
MR3
MR2
103:50
MR1
MS1
MS2
MS3
1541.50
1456.50
1,554.94
1,549.76
1,523.82
1,520.62
1,514.20
1,500.63
1,487.05
1,483.84
1,480.63
1,477.43
1,460.00
IE ES HAS MADE A BULLISH BREAKOUT ON THE MONTH
OOK TO BUY THE FIRST RETRACEMENT. SUPPORT WILL
CK IN AS THE ES APPROACHES THE ZT PIVOT IN WHITE
ID THE MIDPOINT OF THE PERSISTENCE ZONE
RANGE DASHED LINE.
ESH13 FAILED TO MAKE A BEARISH BREAKOUT ON
THE MONTH NO CANDLE BODY CLOSE BELOW THE
MIDPOINT BETWEEN MS1 AND MS2 GENERATING A
BUY SIGNAL FROM RULE 8 AS WE EXPECT THE ES TO
REVERT BACK TO THE ZT PIVOT AND TO POSSIBLY ATTEMPT
TO MAKE A BULLISH BREAKOUT. THE BEARS ALSO FAILED TO
TAKE CONTROL OF THE MARKET TIME FILTER DID NOT HOLD
BELOW BOTTOM OF THE PZ.
THIS PROVIDED ALIGNMENT BETWEEN THE DIRECTIONAL
AND CONTROL BIAS WHICH INCREASES THE PROBABILITY
OF WINNING.

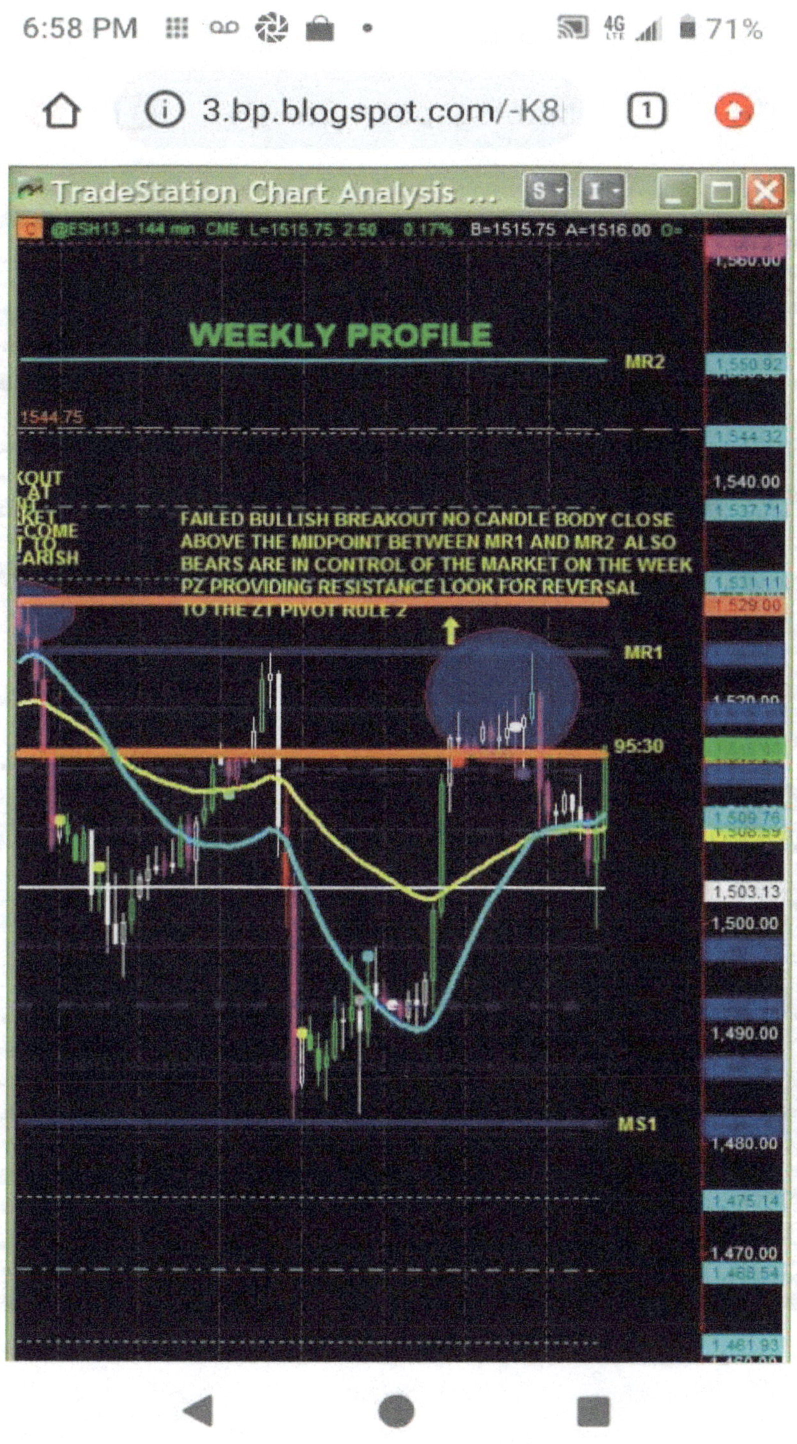
6:58 PM
71%
3.bp.blogspot.com/-K8
TradeStation Chart Analysis ...
@ESH13 - 144 min CME L=1515.75 2.50 0.17% B=1515.75 A=1516.00
WEEKLY PROFILE
MR2
1544.75
FAILED BULLISH BREAKOUT NO CANDLE BODY CLOSE
ABOVE THE MIDPOINT BETWEEN MR1 AND MR2 ALSO
BEARS ARE IN CONTROL OF THE MARKET ON THE WEEK
PZ PROVIDING RESISTANCE LOOK FOR REVERSAL
TO THE ZT PIVOT RULE 2
MR1
95:30
MS1
1,550.92
1,544.32
1,540.00
1,537.71
1,531.11
1,529.00
1,509.76
1,503.13
1,500.00
1,490.00
1,480.00
1,475.14
1,470.00
1,468.54
1,461.93

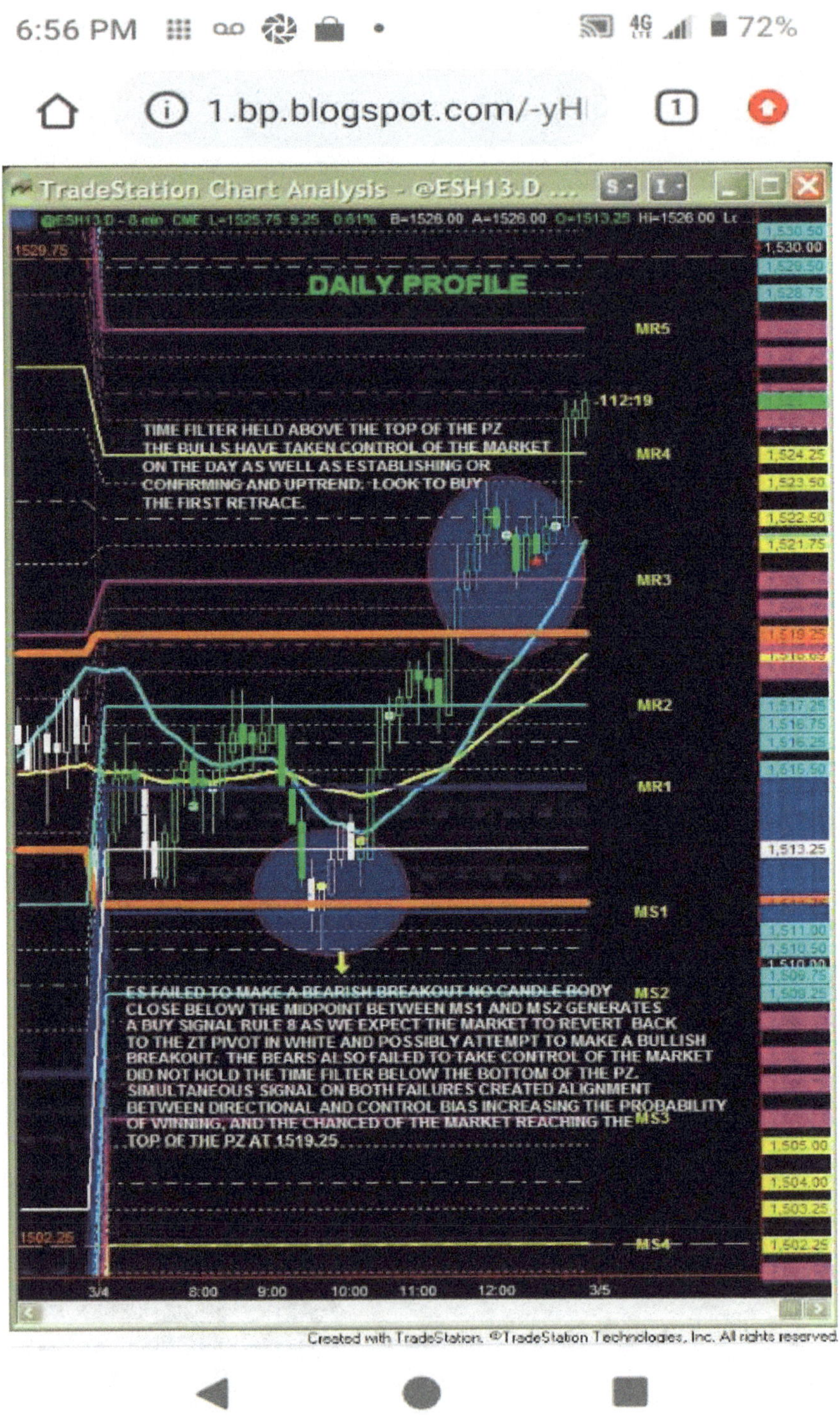
6:56 PM
72%
1.bp.blogspot.com/-yH
TradeStation Chart Analysis - @ESH13.D ...
DAILY PROFILE
MR5
-112:19
TIME FILTER HELD ABOVE THE TOP OF THE PZ
THE BULLS HAVE TAKEN CONTROL OF THE MARKET
ON THE DAY AS WELL AS ESTABLISHING OR
CONFIRMING AND UPTREND. LOOK TO BUY
THE FIRST RETRACE.
MR4
MR3
MR2
MR1
MS1
ES FAILED TO MAKE A BEARISH BREAKOUT NO CANDLE BODY
CLOSE BELOW THE MIDPOINT BETWEEN MS1 AND MS2 GENERATES
A BUY SIGNAL RULE 8 AS WE EXPECT THE MARKET TO REVERT BACK
TO THE ZT PIVOT IN WHITE AND POSSIBLY ATTEMPT TO MAKE A BULLISH
BREAKOUT. THE BEARS ALSO FAILED TO TAKE CONTROL OF THE MARKET
DID NOT HOLD THE TIME FILTER BELOW THE BOTTOM OF THE PZ.
SIMULTANEOUS SIGNAL ON BOTH FAILURES CREATED ALIGNMENT
BETWEEN DIRECTIONAL AND CONTROL BIAS INCREASING THE PROBABILITY
OF WINNING, AND THE CHANCED OF THE MARKET REACHING THE
TOP OF THE PZ AT 1519.25
MS2
MS3
MS4
1529.75
1502.25
1,530.00
1,524.25
1,523.50
1,522.50
1,521.75
1,513.25
1,505.00
1,504.00
1,503.25
1,502.25
3/4
8:00
9:00
10:00
11:00
12:00
3/5
Created with TradeStation. ©TradeStation Technologies, Inc. All rights reserved.

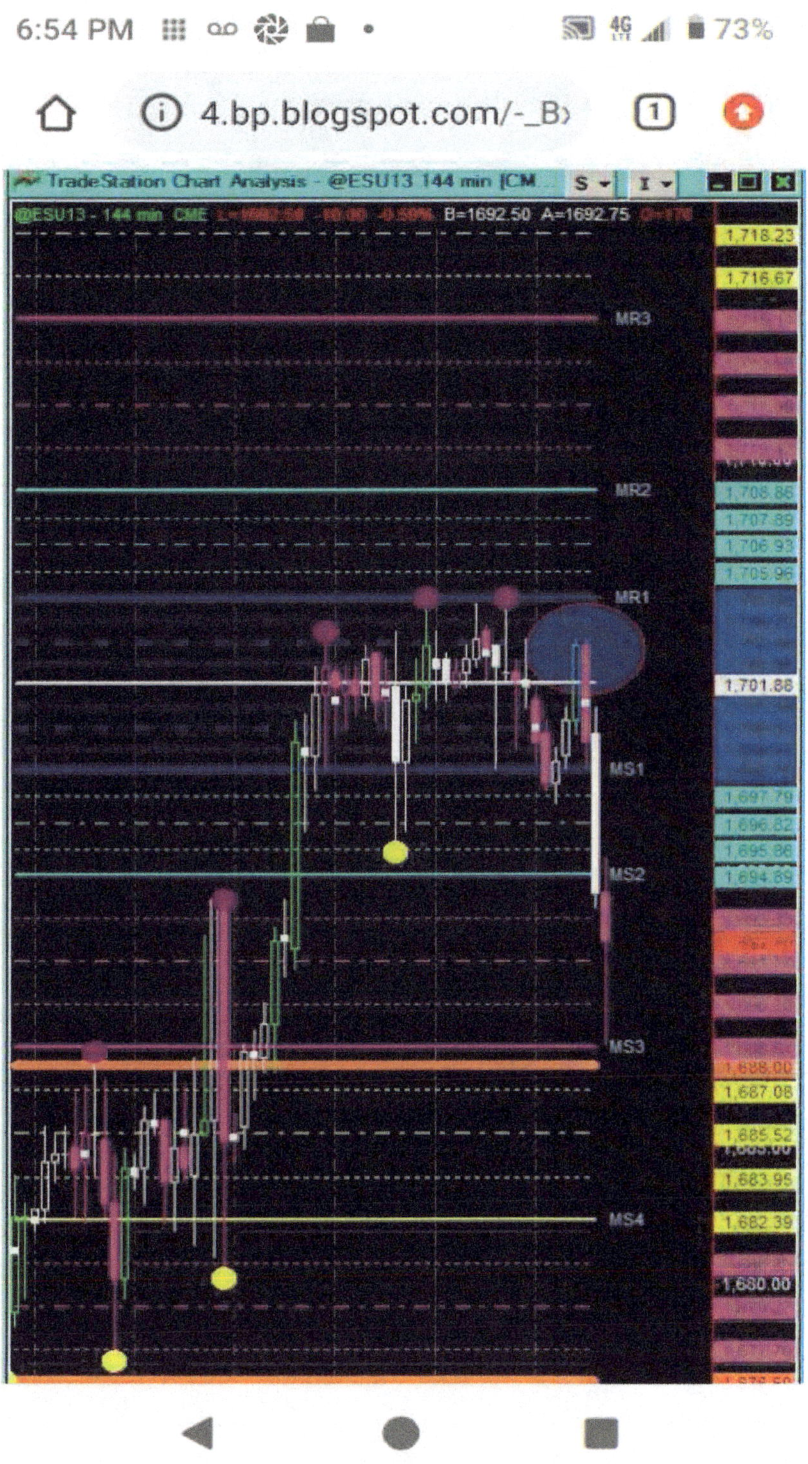
6:54 PM
73%
4.bp.blogspot.com/-_B›
TradeStation Chart Analysis - @ESU13 144 min [CM
@ESU13 - 144 min CME
B=1692.50 A=1692.75
MR3
MR2
MR1
MS1
MS2
MS3
MS4
1,718.23
1,716.67
1,708.86
1,707.89
1,706.93
1,705.96
1,701.86
1,697.79
1,696.82
1,695.86
1,694.89
1,688.00
1,687.08
1,685.52
1,683.95
1,682.39
1,680.00

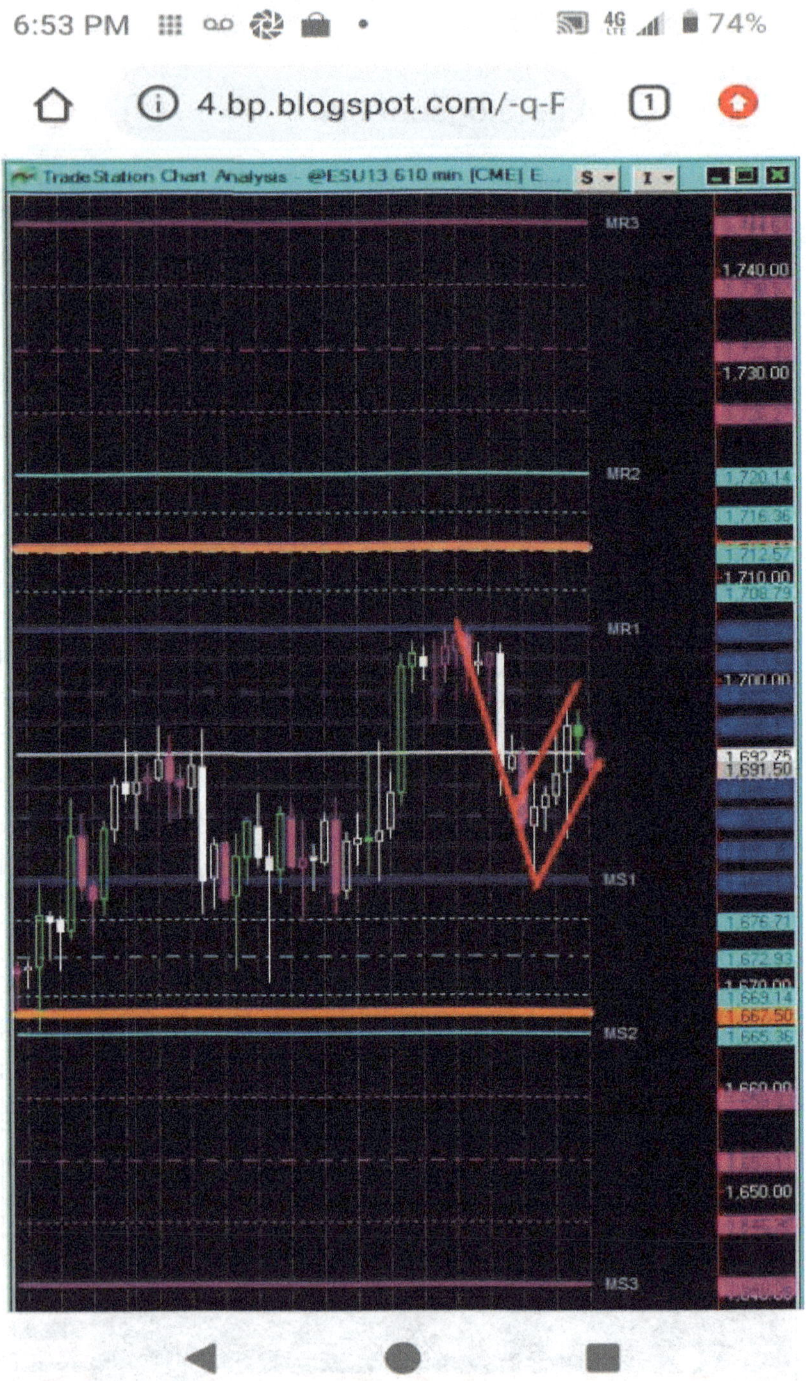
6:53 PM
74%
4.bp.blogspot.com/-q-F
TradeStation Chart Analysis - @ESU13 610 min [CME] E
MR3
1,740.00
1,730.00
MR2
1,720.14
1,716.36
1,712.57
1,710.00
1,708.79
MR1
1,700.00
1,692.75
1,691.50
MS1
1,676.71
1,672.93
1,670.00
1,669.14
1,667.50
MS2
1,665.36
1,660.00
1,650.00
MS3

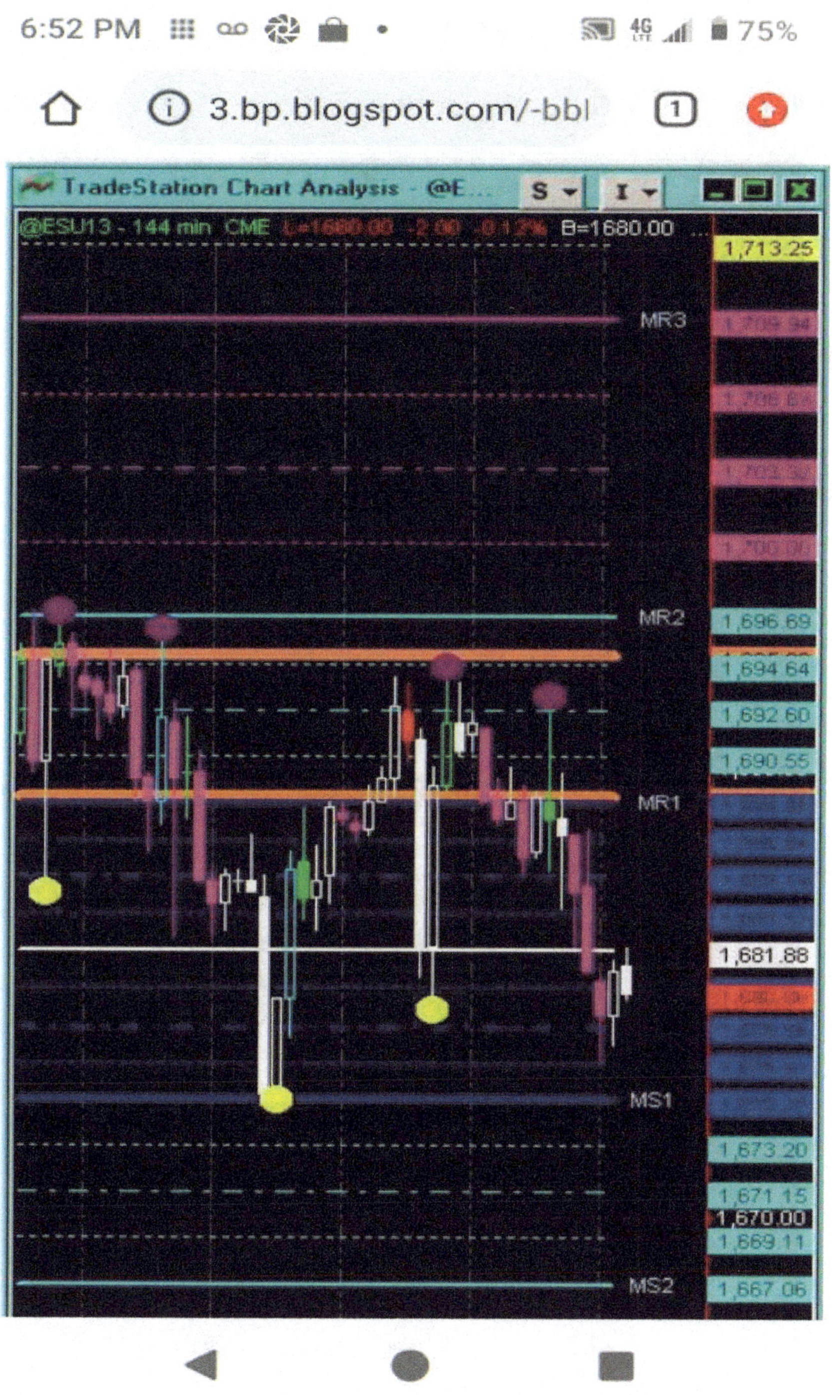
6:52 PM
75%
3.bp.blogspot.com/-bbl
TradeStation Chart Analysis - @E...
@ESU13 - 144 min CME
B=1680.00
1,713.25
MR3
MR2
1,696.69
1,694.64
1,692.60
1,690.55
MR1
1,681.88
MS1
1,673.20
1,671.15
1,670.00
1,669.11
MS2
1,667.06

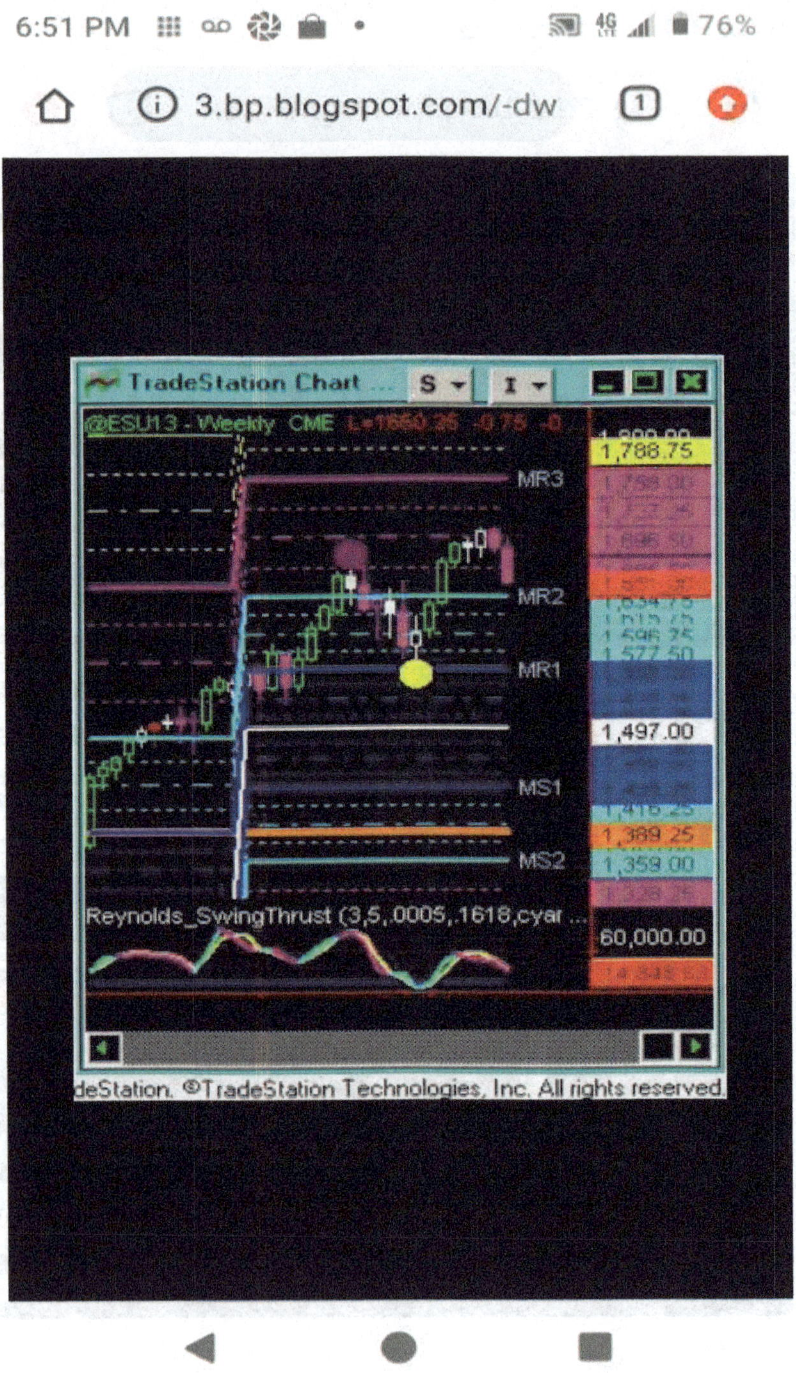
6:51 PM
76%
3.bp.blogspot.com/-dw
TradeStation Chart ...
@ESU13 - Weekly CME
1,788.75
MR3
MR2
MR1
1,497.00
MS1
1,389.25
MS2
1,359.00
Reynolds_SwingThrust (3,5,.0005,.1618,cyar ...
60,000.00
deStation. ©TradeStation Technologies, Inc. All rights reserved.

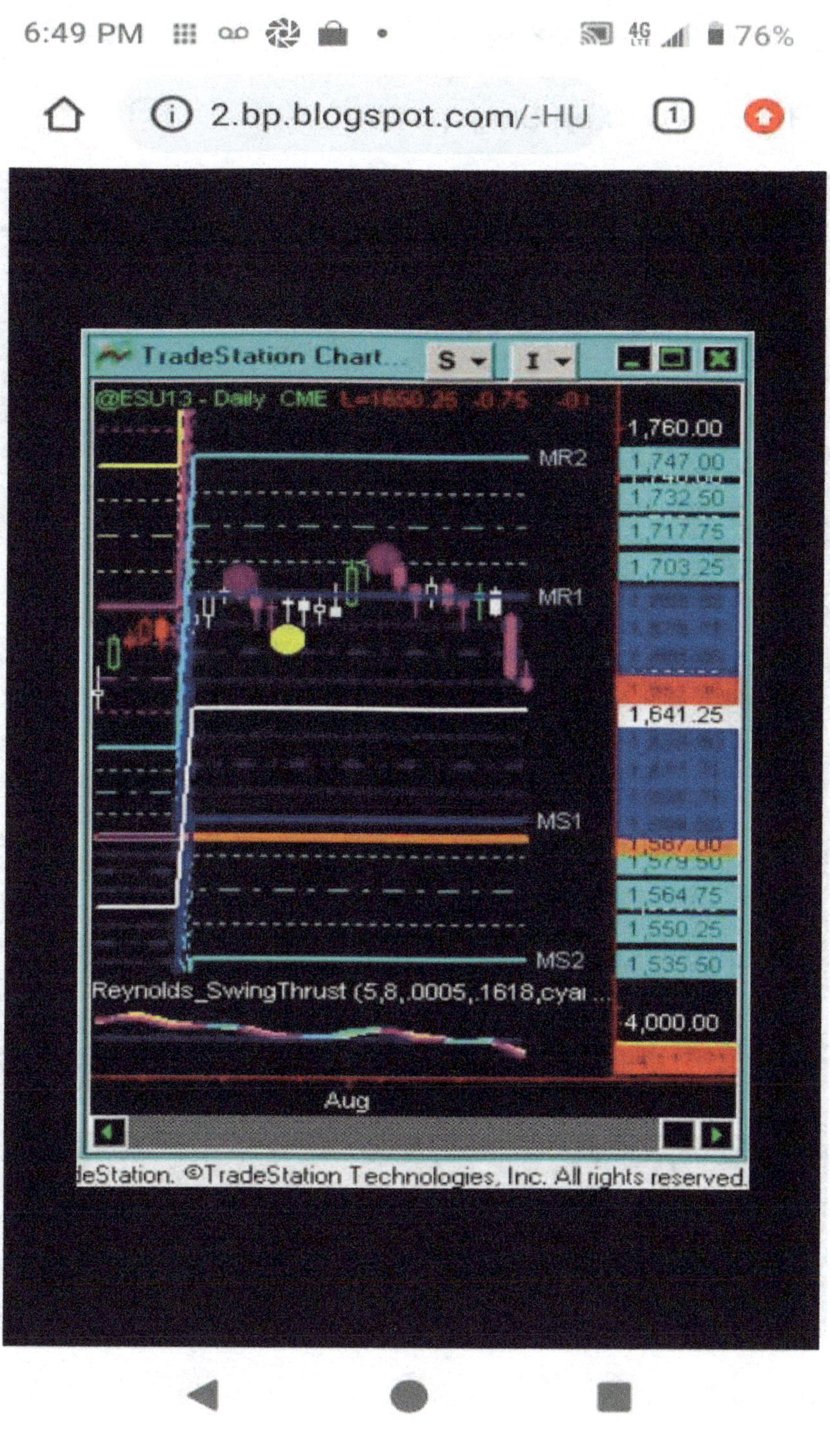
6:49 PM
76%
2.bp.blogspot.com/-HU
TradeStation Chart...
@ESU13 - Daily CME
MR2
MR1
MS1
MS2
1,760.00
1,747.00
1,732.50
1,717.75
1,703.25
1,641.25
1,579.50
1,564.75
1,550.25
1,535.50
Reynolds_SwingThrust (5,8,.0005,.1618,cyai ...
4,000.00
Aug
deStation. ©TradeStation Technologies, Inc. All rights reserved.

6:48 PM
77%
3.bp.blogspot.com/-dw
TradeStation Chart ...
S
I
@ESU13 - Weekly CME
1,788.75
MR3
MR2
MR1
1,497.00
MS1
1,389.25
MS2
1,359.00
Reynolds_SwingThrust (3,5,.0005,.1618,cyar ...
60,000.00
deStation. ©TradeStation Technologies, Inc. All rights reserved.

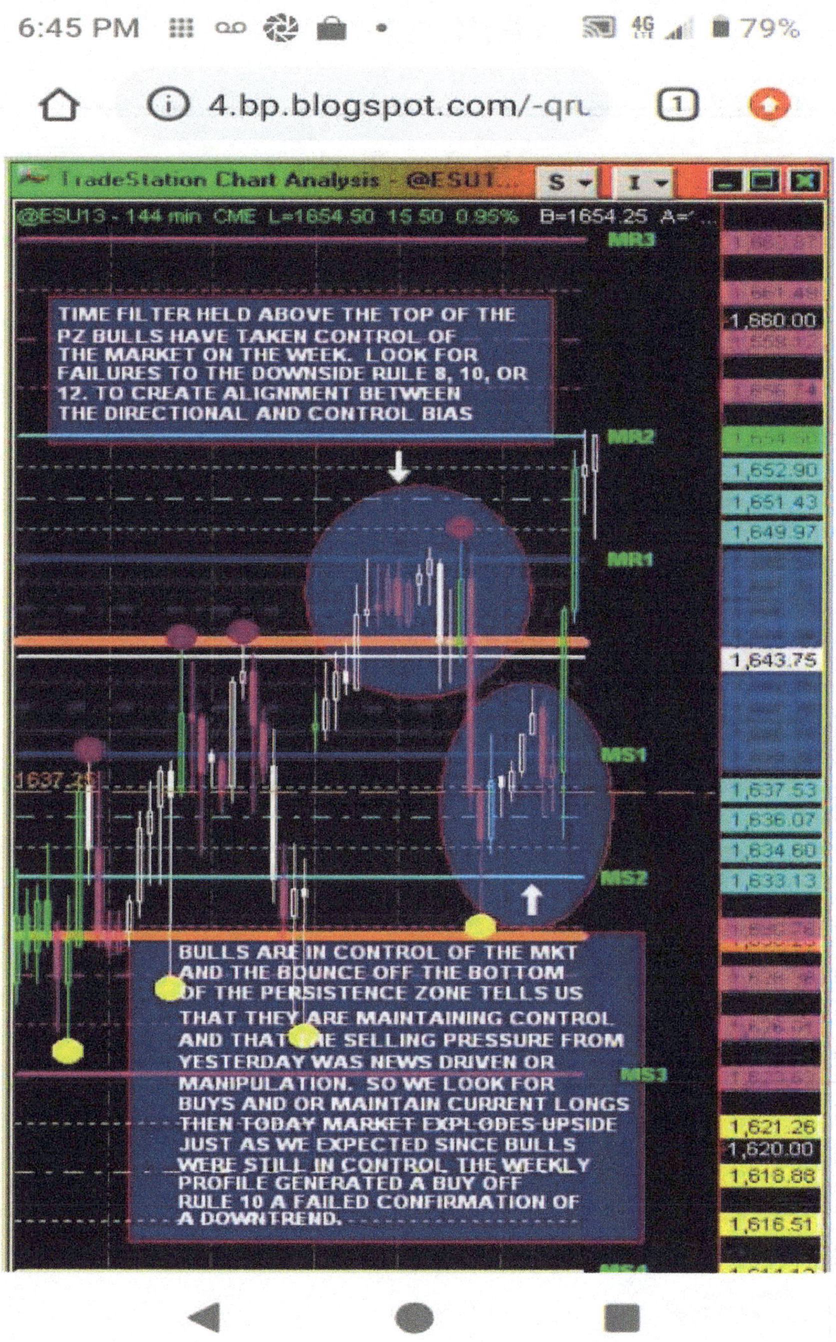
6:45 PM
79%
4.bp.blogspot.com/-qru
TradeStation Chart Analysis - @ESU1...
@ESU13 - 144 min CME L=1654.50 15.50 0.95% B=1654.25 A=...
MR3
TIME FILTER HELD ABOVE THE TOP OF THE PZ BULLS HAVE TAKEN CONTROL OF THE MARKET ON THE WEEK. LOOK FOR FAILURES TO THE DOWNSIDE RULE 8, 10, OR 12. TO CREATE ALIGNMENT BETWEEN THE DIRECTIONAL AND CONTROL BIAS
1,660.00
MR2
1,652.90
1,651.43
1,649.97
MR1
1,643.75
MS1
1637.25
1,637.53
1,636.07
1,634.60
MS2
1,633.13
BULLS ARE IN CONTROL OF THE MKT AND THE BOUNCE OFF THE BOTTOM OF THE PERSISTENCE ZONE TELLS US THAT THEY ARE MAINTAINING CONTROL AND THAT THE SELLING PRESSURE FROM YESTERDAY WAS NEWS DRIVEN OR MANIPULATION. SO WE LOOK FOR BUYS AND OR MAINTAIN CURRENT LONGS THEN TODAY MARKET EXPLODES UPSIDE JUST AS WE EXPECTED SINCE BULLS WERE STILL IN CONTROL THE WEEKLY PROFILE GENERATED A BUY OFF RULE 10 A FAILED CONFIRMATION OF A DOWNTREND.
MS3
1,621.26
1,620.00
1,618.88
1,616.51

APPENDIX B

The Zone-Trader

Derived from Support/Resistance Levels

The Zone-Trader is a predefined market arena for day-trading that seeks to utilize intraday trading action in order to determine future market direction. Each zone is numbered and specifically labeled in order to profile and interpret the condition of the market and give the trader a specific description of where the market is and what it is trying to do.

The Zone-Trader accomplishes this by analyzing the integrals of the market (volume, open interest, volatility, range, and trend) as the market moves from zone to zone throughout intraday trading. By understanding the condition of the market as derived by The Zone-Trader and combining that knowledge with the analysis of the integrals, the day-trader will be able to develop or enhance their trading strategies.

The Zone-Trader also seeks to optimize the entry points for intraday trade which is the key element for maximizing profit potential.

The potential for profit that is offered by each market is another key element. If the current market has a small intraday range and a lack of liquidity then the trader should change markets. However, if the market presents a large intraday range and high volume, therefore providing profit potential and the trader fails at being successful then they must change their trading methods or strategies. This is the underlying principle for the creation of The Zone-Trader.

The Zone-Trader is designed to be applied to auction markets where price is derived from the negotiation among market participants.

The market has three conditions: balanced, trending, or transitioning. The Zone-Trader seeks to profile the market and provide the day trader with a description that determines one of these conditions.

As the market moves from balanced to attempting to reverse, to trending and back to balance The Zone-Trader will profile these movements. This will enhance the performance of the trader's methodologies by providing sentiment and reducing emotions.

DERIVATIVE CONCEPTS INC. original proprietary formula for deriving intraday support and resistance levels in the underlying instrument that leads to the construction of the zones.

The next level will be the profiling method derived from The Zone-Trader and will continue to enhance the trader's current methodologies and strategies as well as reduce the impact that one's emotions can play upon intraday trading decisions and entry prices.

The Zone-Trader is partitioned into 13 Zones using support and resistance levels. Each zone is also named, relative to the anticipated movement of the market price action.

The Zones are numbered in a back and forth pattern. Bullish zones are designated by even numbers and bearish zones are designated by odd numbers.

These zones are shown in the following table.

DERIVATIVE CONCEPTS INC.

7635 Avila Drive
Sparks, NV 89436
www.DerivativeConceptsInc.com

Matt Reynolds
626-808-7546
derivativeconceptsinc@gmail.com

DCI004A4.00.doc
Revision:Ø 02/26/2007 -1- Prepared by Doug Wheeler

The Zone-Trader Zones

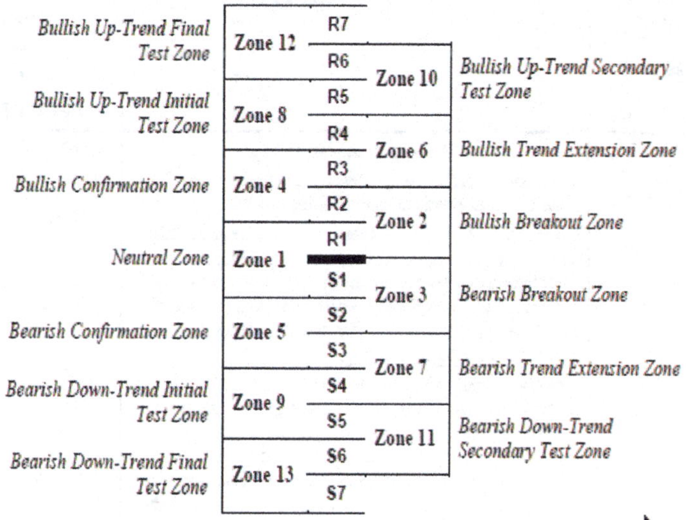

DERIVATIVE CONCEPTS INC.

7635 Avila Drive
Sparks, NV 89436
www.DerivativeConceptsInc.com

Matt Reynolds
626-808-7546
derivativeconceptsinc@gmail.com

Price Movement Up ⬆ Bullish Trend	ZONE DESCRIPTION	Price Movement Down ⬇ Bearish Trend
Zone 1 (S1 to R1) *Neutral Zone*	This is the *Neutral Zone* for intraday trade. The market is said to be in balance while trading within Zone 1 with an equal amount of buying and selling. On days prior to a major economic data release and at times when the market approaches key long-term Fibonacci Retracements we tend to see the market close within Zone 1 becoming balanced prior to the new data, or in the case of Fibs prior to position traders re-entering the market. The wider the difference of Zone 1 (S1 – R1), the more range-bound the trading will become for that day, with multiple reverses off the S/R computed prices. Shorter or condensed Zone 1 ranges, increase the likelihood of a breakout occurring and the development of a trending day. This is especially useful if the tight Zone 1 range occurs on a day that has been given a strong sentiment reading by the market scenario. The trader will look to buy or sell depending upon the sentiment (bullish or bearish) on a stop one tick above R1 or one tick below S1.	**Zone 1** (R1 to S1) *Neutral Zone*

DERIVATIVE CONCEPTS INC.

7635 Avila Drive
Sparks, NV 89436
www.DerivativeConceptsInc.com

Matt Reynolds
626-808-7546
derivativeconceptsinc@gmail.com

Price Movement Up ⬆ Bullish Trend	ZONE DESCRIPTION	Price Movement Down ⬇ Bearish Trend
Zone 2 (R1 to R2) *Bullish Breakout Zone*	This is the *Bullish* or *Bearish Breakout Zone*. For an anticipated up trend, the market will have to trade completely through Zone 2 making a cross of R2 into Zone 4 in order to establish a bullish sentiment for the day and attempt to develop an up trend. If the market is unable to penetrate R2 look for a reversal back into the neutral area of Zone 1. For an anticipated down trend, the market will have to trade completely through Zone 3 making a cross of S2 into Zone 5 in order to establish a bearish sentiment for the day and attempt to develop a down trend. If the market is unable to penetrate S2 look for a reversal back into the neutral area of Zone 1. **Note:** Zones 2 & 3 will always have the smallest ranges in comparison to all other Zones as they serve to be the distance that market will have to travel above or below the neutral zone in order to establish a sentiment for the day. Zone 2 & 3 are the first standard deviation within the normal distribution of the S/R Levels Formula.	**Zone 3** (S1 to S2) *Bearish Breakout Zone*

Price Movement Up ⬆ Bullish Trend	ZONE DESCRIPTION	Price Movement Down ⬇ Bearish Trend
Zone 4 (R2 to R3) *Bullish Confirmation Zone*	This is the *Bullish* or *Bearish Confirmation Zone*. The market is attempting to transition from balanced to trending. For an up trend condition, if the market trades at or above R2 for a time period of 7 consecutive minutes, then the confirmation is established and the trader will look for a bullish trend to develop. As the bullish trend develops, the market will attempt to breakout out of Zone 4 and continue to extend the trend. For a down trend condition, if the market trades at or below S2 for a time period of 7 consecutive minutes, then the confirmation is established and the trader will look for a bearish trend to develop. As the bearish trend develops, the market will attempt to breakout out of Zone 5 and continue to extend the trend. **Note:** Zones 4 & 5 are the second deviation from the neutral area and the market must trade within these zones for the specified time period, on a consecutive basis, in order to establish a sentiment for the day. The trader will also note if the market closes within one of these zones, as it would then be applicable to the next day's trading. If the market breaks out of either of these zones it will be attempting to extend the trend. If this occurs, this will be the underlying basis for the description of the next two zones.	**Zone 5** (S2 to S3) *Bearish Confirmation Zone*

Price Movement Up ⬆ Bullish Trend	ZONE DESCRIPTION	Price Movement Down ⬇ Bearish Trend
Zone 6 (R3 to R4) *Bullish Trend Extension Zone*	This is the *Bullish* or *Bearish Trend Extension Zone*. The market is trending. This zone functions as the one of the tails of error within the bell distribution. For an up trend, the market must break-out of Zone 6 in order to extend the bullish trend. The trader will look for the market to test R4 and attempt to break this price level. At this point, the trader should see strong resistance at R4 as the market fights to transition back into a balanced state. For a down trend, the market must break-out of Zone 7 in order to extend the bearish trend. The trader will look for the market to test S4 and attempt to break this price level. At this point, the trader should see strong support at S4 as the market fights to transition back into a balanced state. *(continued next page)*	**Zone 7** (S3 to S4) *Bearish Trend Extension Zone*

Price Movement Up ⬆ Bullish Trend	ZONE DESCRIPTION	Price Movement Down ⬇ Bearish Trend
Zone 6 (R3 to R4) *Bullish Trend Extension Zone*	*Bullish or Bearish Trend Extension Zone – continued* **Note:** Zones 6 & 7 will attempt to pull the market back into a balanced state and return it towards the neutral zone prior to the close. These are the tails of the bell distribution and the market is attempting to continue the trend in the current direction. If the market breaks out of either zone and continues to increase the length of the trend, the market will begin to develop multiple quasi shaped distributions. If the market develops more than one quasi bell shaped distribution it has transitioned from being balanced into a trending market. The trader will look for the continuance of the trend the following day and will be able to develop a recognition system that measures the time frames under taken during a trending market, a balanced market, and the transition for one to the other. These *Bullish or Bearish Trend Extension Zone* are key areas for the trader to examine in order to determine the strength of the current trend and the possibility of the continuance of that trend. If the market fails to touch R4 or S4 the trader will look for a reversal and a revision of the prices back towards the neutral area. Likewise, if the trader examines the market progressing through Zone 6 or Zone 7 depending on the current trend, they will then look for the break of R4 or S4. However, if the market touches either of these price levels and bounces off of these support/resistance levels in a rapid motion the trader will look for a reversal. During this market condition keep in mind the rule of 3. If the market tests either of these price levels and bounces off of the levels steadily, then the third test will typically be the determining test and establish the direction. For an up trend, the market will either break into Zone 8 or it will reverse back into Zone 4. For a down trend, the market will either break into Zone 9 or it will reverse back into Zone 5.	**Zone 7** (S3 to S4) *Bearish Trend Extension Zone*

Price Movement Up ⬆ Bullish Trend	ZONE DESCRIPTION	Price Movement Down ⬇ Bearish Trend
Zone 8 (R4 to R5) *Bullish Up-Trend Initial Test Zone*	*Bullish Up-Trend Initial Test-Zone* or *Bearish Down-Trend Initial Test-Zone* This is the first Test-Zone for the now established trend. For an up trend, Zone 8 is where the market will start to become pressured with an increase in selling volume as the market attempts to continue the current bullish trend. So in a sense, Zone 8 is testing the strength of the up trend and is attempting to push the market back towards Zone 6. This is where volume will begin decreasing as the prices within Zone 8 are rejected. For a down trend, Zone 9 is where the market will start to become pressured with an increase in buying volume as the market attempts to continue the current bearish trend. Zone 9 is testing the strength of the down trend and is attempting to push the market back towards Zone 7. This is where volume will begin decreasing as the prices within Zone 9 are rejected. The trader will evaluate the strength of the trend. Typical trend indicators used are the Herrick Payoff Index, Aroon, and/or DMI. in combination with the movement of volume and open-interest. For an up trend, if volume is increasing and open interest is decreasing the trader should look for the market to test R5 and attempt to break into Zone 10. If volume is decreasing and open interest is increasing the trader should look for the market to retrace back into Zone 6. For a down trend, if volume is increasing and open interest is increasing the trader should look for the market to test S5 and attempt to break into Zone 13. If volume is decreasing and open interest is decreasing the trader should look for the market to retrace back into Zone 7. *(continued next page)*	**Zone 9** (S4 to S5) *Bearish Down-Trend Initial Test Zone*

7635 Avila Drive
Sparks, NV 89436
www.DerivativeConceptsInc.com

Matt Reynolds
626-808-7546
derivativeconceptsinc@gmail.com

Price Movement Up ⬆ **Bullish Trend**	**ZONE DESCRIPTION**	**Price Movement Down** ⬇ **Bearish Trend**
Zone 8 (R4 to R5) *Bullish Up-Trend Initial Test Zone*	*Bullish Up-Trend Initial Test-Zone* or *Bearish Down-Trend Initial Test-Zone – continued* Note: Zones 8 & 9 are the first Test-Zones and every subsequent Zone from this point on will all be a Test-Zone as the market attempts to continue and progress with the now established trend, whether bullish or bearish. All Test-Zones function in the same manner. As the Zone gets further from the Neutral Zone (i.e. the Zone number increases), the strength of the resistance or support also increases as well.	**Zone 9** (S4 to S5) *Bearish Down-Trend Initial Test Zone*
Zone 10 (R5 to R6) *Bullish Up-Trend Secondary Test Zone*	*Bullish Up-Trend Secondary Test Zone* or *Bearish Down-Trend Secondary Test Zone.* This is the second Test-Zone for the trend. For a bullish up trend, Zone 10 functions in the same manner as Zone 8 but with higher resistance strength. For a bearish down trend, Zone 11 functions in the same manner as Zone 9 but with higher support strength.	**Zone 11** (S5 to S6) *Bearish Down-Trend Secondary Test Zone*
Zone 12 (R6 to R7) *Bullish Up-Trend Final Test Zone*	*Bullish Up-Trend Final Test-Zone* or *Bearish Down-Trend Final Test-Zone.* For a bullish up trend, Zone 12 functions in the same manner as Zone 10 but with very high resistance strength. For a bearish down trend, Zone 13 functions in the same manner as Zone 11 but with very high support strength.	**Zone 13** (S6 to S7) *Bearish Down-Trend Final Test Zone*

DERIVATIVE CONCEPTS INC.

7635 Avila Drive
Sparks, NV 89436
www.DerivativeConceptsInc.com

Matt Reynolds
626-808-7546
derivativeconceptsinc@gmail.com

Using Zone-Trader

Once you become a Zone-Trader you will need to track three key elements on a day-to-day basis after the close of the market. These three elements are:

- Persistence Zone
- Rejection Zone
- Closing Zone

Utilize day session data for evaluating and determining these elements.

These elements are a key feature of the Zone-Trader. A trader will use these elements in order to track the market as it moves from balanced to transitioning to trending and back again.

For example, consider the following hypothetical scenario. The first day the market is up-trending and during intraday trading the market gets rejected by Zone 6 The Bullish Trend Extension Zone, and closes back in Zone 4 or Zone 2. Then the second (following) day the market opens and trades up to R2 and attempts to move into Zone 4 The Bullish Trend Confirmation Zone, but gets rejected and closes lower in Zone 2. This would signal the trader that the market is beginning to transition from a trending market back to a balanced market. The trader looks for some type of retracement within the next couple of trading days as the market becomes balanced. Once the retracement occurs the trader will see the market get rejected by one of the bearish zones and close back in the Neutral Zone, thus signaling that the market has become balanced again.

Persistence Zone

The Zone-Trader uses **time** in order to determine the Persistence Zone. The Persistence Zone utilizes day session data, on a time chart (i.e. day-to-day basis).
For example, the trader should consider using a time period chart set at one minute in order to perform this analysis.

The Zone-Trader depicts the Zone that the market trades within for the longest period of non-continuous time as the Persistence Zone. The trader simply determines the zones that visually appears to contain the most candles (or bars), which is usually three zones or less intraday, and then counts the candles within each Zone. Note that when determining which zone a candle is in, the body is typically more important than the wicks (i.e. the open-to-close range of the bar).

The Zone with the most candles (or bars) identifies the **Persistence Zone** for the next days trading. The trader will either note the zone top and bottom price levels, or can draw extended lines across their chart.

The Zone-Trader uses time because of the fact that wherever the market trades for the longest period of time is where the battle starts between the bulls and the bears on an intraday basis. This Persistence Zone will act as a magnet the following day trying to pull the market back within this zone range.

To be clear here, once the trader has determined what Zone establishes the Persistence Zone take note of the name of that Zone and then write down the price levels that created it.

For example, if the Persistence Zone is determined to be Zone 2 The Bullish Breakout Zone, then you will note that the fight was even between the bulls and the bears within Zone 2 as the market was attempting to break into an uptrend on an intraday basis. Then you will want to write down the prices of R1 and R2 which are the levels that create Zone 2. The next trading day you will want to draw or plot these demarcation price lines of the Persistence Zone on your chart.

For an up trend, the market must trade completely through the Persistence Zone in the bearish direction in order to stop the up trend and attempt to start a transition back to a balanced market.

For a down trend, the market must trade completely through the Persistence Zone in the bullish direction in order to stop the down trend and attempt to start a transition back to a balanced market.

Rejection Zone

For determining the Rejection Zone, the Zone-Trader just simply tracks which Zone or zones are rejected by the market on an intraday basis. As described previously, this will be a useful for the trader to track the markets movement from balanced-to-transitioning-to-trending, and so forth.

For example, if the market gets rejected by Zone 4 the trader will acknowledge that the market had a bullish breakout by trading through Zone 2 and breaking R2, but failed to establish an up trend due to the market being rejected by the Bullish Trend Confirmation Zone. Do not be surprised to see the market start to become range-bound or retrace in the next couple of trading days.

The more that a trader applies the Rejection Zone they will begin to observe patterns where the market tends to repeat itself.

For example, the market may get rejected by Zone 6 The Bullish Trend Extension Zone. Then on the following trading day the Rejection Zone may be Zone 4. This will signal that the market confirmed an up trend the first day, but failed to extend it on that day. Then on the second day the market failed to confirm the up trend. This implies that the market may be reaching a top, or is transitioning back towards a balanced market.

Closing Zone

For determining the Closing Zone, the Zone-Trader just simply acknowledges what Zone the market closes in, based off of intraday data on a day-to-day basis. As previously described this is of importance to track the movement of the market and can provide useful knowledge of an upcoming retracement or breakout.

If the market closes within the Neutral Zone it is said to be in balance and the trader will see range-bound trading on an intraday basis as the bulls and the bears fight to control the future direction of prices.

Market Movement Probabilities

The Zone-Trader provides numerous possibilities when used with probability and statistical analysis.

The specific intraday trading zones definitively establishes the current market action, with indications of future or probable market actions. When a trader tracks the trading zones with the actual outcome, the probability of a particular market action can then also be established.

DERIVATIVE CONCEPTS INC.

7635 Avila Drive
Sparks, NV 89436
www.DerivativeConceptsInc.com

Matt Reynolds
626-808-7546
derivativeconceptsinc@gmail.com

By performing probability and other statistically based analysis, the trader has an even further advantage in participating in winning trades.

For example, if the market closes within Zone 1 The Neutral Zone, then the Trader knows that the market is in a balanced state. Statistically the Trader can then determine how long the market might remain in a balanced state before the market begins to transition back to a trending market.

If the market is up-trending and closes in Zone 6 The Bullish Trend Extension Zone, the Trader can determine the probability of the market hitting R2 the following day, if the market continues to remain in a trending state.

Combining the Zone-Trader with probability and statistical analysis will open a whole new realm for the trading world with endless possibilities.

Summary

The Zone-Trader is revolutionary due to the creation and naming of the individual zones. For the first time the Trader can determine where the market is and what the market is trying to do throughout a day session.

The Zone-Trader increases the Trader's ability to track the market from balanced-to-transitioning-to-trending through the use of the three key elements: Persistence Zone, Rejection Zone, Closing Zone.

A trader that is using The Zone-Trader methodology is provided with a trading advantage. This is due to the ability of Zone-Trader to provide the Trader with signals of upcoming changes in the state of the market (i.e. balanced, transitioning, trending).

7635 Avila Drive
Sparks, NV 89436
www.DerivativeConceptsInc.com

Matt Reynolds
626-808-7546
derivativeconceptsinc@gmail.com

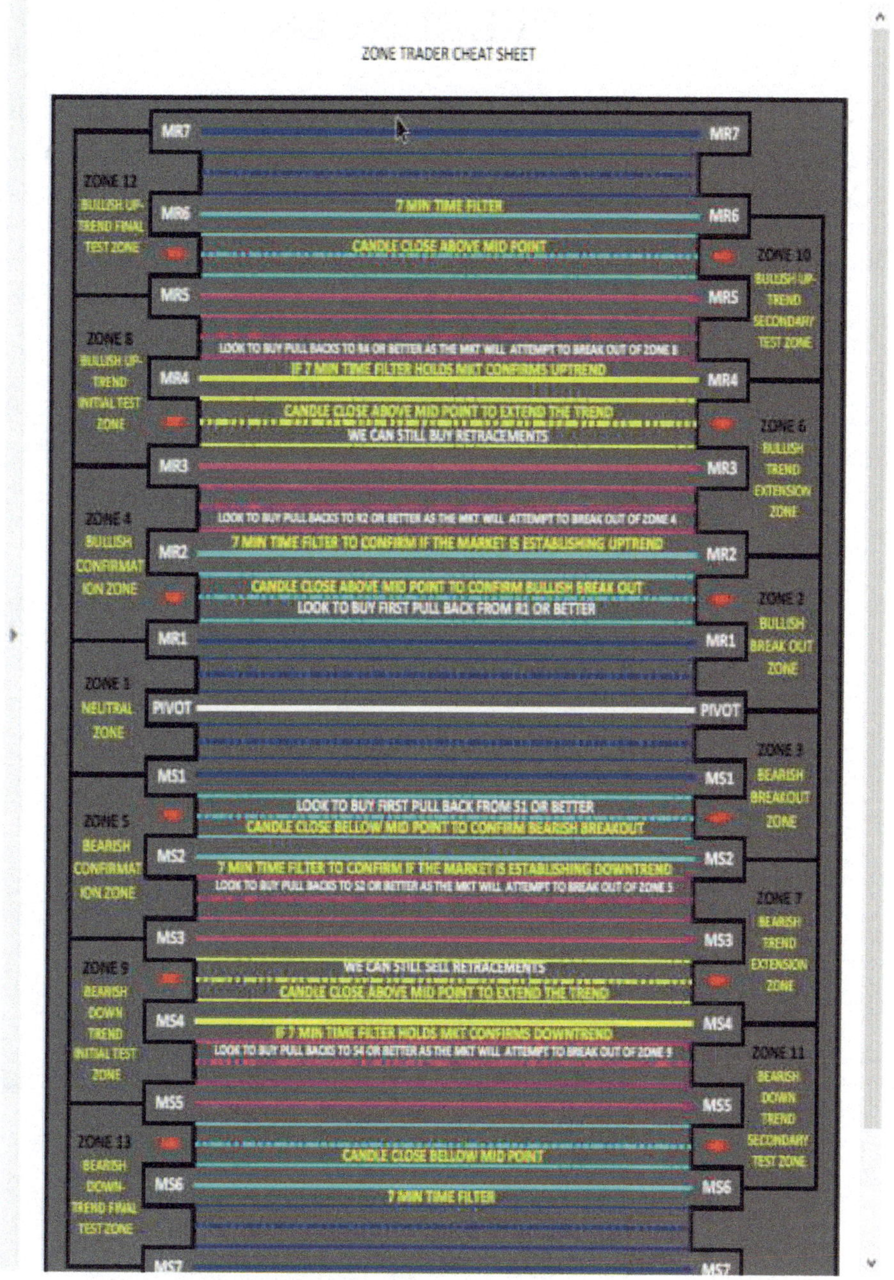
ZONE TRADER CHEAT SHEET
MR7
ZONE 12
BULLISH UP-TREND FINAL TEST ZONE
MR6
7 MIN TIME FILTER
CANDLE CLOSE ABOVE MID POINT
ZONE 10
BULLISH UP-TREND SECONDARY TEST ZONE
MR5
ZONE 8
BULLISH UP-TREND INITIAL TEST ZONE
LOOK TO BUY PULL BACKS TO R4 OR BETTER AS THE MKT WILL ATTEMPT TO BREAK OUT OF ZONE 8
MR4
IF 7 MIN TIME FILTER HOLDS MKT CONFIRMS UPTREND
CANDLE CLOSE ABOVE MID POINT TO EXTEND THE TREND
WE CAN STILL BUY RETRACEMENTS
ZONE 6
BULLISH TREND EXTENSION ZONE
MR3
ZONE 4
BULLISH CONFIRMATION ZONE
LOOK TO BUY PULL BACKS TO R2 OR BETTER AS THE MKT WILL ATTEMPT TO BREAK OUT OF ZONE 4
MR2
7 MIN TIME FILTER TO CONFIRM IF THE MARKET IS ESTABLISHING UPTREND
CANDLE CLOSE ABOVE MID POINT TO CONFIRM BULLISH BREAK OUT
LOOK TO BUY FIRST PULL BACK FROM R1 OR BETTER
ZONE 2
BULLISH BREAK OUT ZONE
MR1
ZONE 1
NEUTRAL ZONE
PIVOT
ZONE 3
BEARISH BREAKOUT ZONE
MS1
LOOK TO BUY FIRST PULL BACK FROM S1 OR BETTER
CANDLE CLOSE BELLOW MID POINT TO CONFIRM BEARISH BREAKOUT
ZONE 5
BEARISH CONFIRMATION ZONE
MS2
7 MIN TIME FILTER TO CONFIRM IF THE MARKET IS ESTABLISHING DOWNTREND
LOOK TO BUY PULL BACKS TO S2 OR BETTER AS THE MKT WILL ATTEMPT TO BREAK OUT OF ZONE 5
ZONE 7
BEARISH TREND EXTENSION ZONE
MS3
ZONE 9
BEARISH DOWN TREND INITIAL TEST ZONE
WE CAN STILL SELL RETRACEMENTS
CANDLE CLOSE ABOVE MID POINT TO EXTEND THE TREND
MS4
IF 7 MIN TIME FILTER HOLDS MKT CONFIRMS DOWNTREND
LOOK TO BUY PULL BACKS TO S4 OR BETTER AS THE MKT WILL ATTEMPT TO BREAK OUT OF ZONE 9
ZONE 11
BEARISH DOWN TREND SECONDARY TEST ZONE
MS5
ZONE 13
BEARISH DOWN-TREND FINAL TEST ZONE
CANDLE CLOSE BELLOW MID POINT
MS6
7 MIN TIME FILTER
MS7

REFERENCES

Mark B. Fisher, August 14, (2002). The Logical Trader: Applying a Method to the Madness (John Wiley and Sons) 1st Edition, New York, NY.

https://www.investopedia.com/terms/f/fibonaccilines.asp

Made in the USA
Monee, IL
03 November 2026

67378087R00075